James William Black

Maryland's Attitude in the Struggle for Canada

Tenth Series

James William Black

Maryland's Attitude in the Struggle for Canada
Tenth Series

ISBN/EAN: 9783337190545

Printed in Europe, USA, Canada, Australia, Japan

Cover: Foto ©ninafisch / pixelio.de

More available books at **www.hansebooks.com**

VII

Maryland's Attitude in the Struggle for Canada

JOHNS HOPKINS UNIVERSITY STUDIES

IN

HISTORICAL AND POLITICAL SCIENCE

HERBERT B. ADAMS, Editor

History is past Politics and Politics present History.—*Freeman*

TENTH SERIES

VII

Maryland's Attitude in the Struggle for Canada

By J. WILLIAM BLACK, Ph. D.

Associate Professor of Political Economy, Oberlin College

BALTIMORE
THE JOHNS HOPKINS PRESS
PUBLISHED MONTHLY
July, 1892

PREFACE.

This paper is a study of the attitude of Maryland in the French and Indian War. Maryland failed to do her duty in that great international struggle between the French and English for the possession of North America, and it was chiefly due, first, to the narrow and niggardly policy of the Provincial Assembly, and secondly, to the dissensions of the Province with the Proprietary government for the purpose of limiting and, perhaps, overthrowing Proprietary rule. The recent publication of portions of the Maryland Archives, under the able editorship of Dr. William Hand Browne, has rendered interesting parts of the history of Maryland accessible to students. The Sharpe Correspondence (Vols. I. and II.) covers the period from 1753 to 1761. It contains much valuable information regarding Maryland's policy during the French and Indian War, and helps to explain the motives of her peculiar conduct. It has been my purpose in this paper, therefore, to present briefly the results of a study of the Sharpe Correspondence and the Proceedings of the Assembly during these years, for the purpose of throwing new light upon Maryland politics at that time. Since Maryland's behavior was due largely to disputes with the Proprietary, I have attempted to trace each dispute from its origin, in order to arrive at a correct understanding of the controversies of the time. We shall find that out of what was really a derelict and obstructive policy developed a commendable spirit of resistance in 1765, which led finally to independence. The sources that have been most serviceable to me in this study are:—Archives of Maryland: Correspondence of Governor Sharpe, Vols. I. and II.; Assembly Proceedings, first three volumes of Archives, and especially the Journals of the Lower House between 1753–1758; Council Proceedings, 1692–1694; Bacon, Laws of Maryland, 1637–1765; Pennsylvania Colonial Records, Vols. VI. and VII.; Dinwiddie Papers, being Vols. III. and IV. of Virginia Historical Society Collections; Franklin's works, and other authorities, references to which are made in the foot-notes.

J. W. B.

CONTENTS.

I. INTRODUCTION:
                             PAGE.
 Maryland a Proprietary Colony........................... 9
 Frederick, Lord Baltimore................................ 10
 Sharpe, Governor of Maryland............................ 11
 Strength and Resources of the Province, Defenses............ 11
 Attitude of the People toward their Government............. 12
 Development of Representative Government................ 12

II. FRENCH AND INDIAN WAR:
 Backwardness of Maryland................................ 15
 French and English Claims................................ 15
 Ohio Company.. 16
 Maryland's Aid requested; Her Inactivity................... 16
 Albany Congress.. 18
 Maryland votes £6000..................................... 19
 Gov. Sharpe proposes a Poll Tax or Stamp Duty............. 20
 Union to be enforced by Parliament........................ 21
 Lack of Unity among the Colonies.......................... 21
 Braddock's Defeat; Danger of the Province................. 24
 The Activity of Other Colonies............................ 25

III. "BONES OF CONTENTION."
 The Assembly vs. the Lord Proprietary..................... 27
 Causes of Maryland's Inactivity............................ 27
 Revenues of the Proprietary: Territorial.................... 27
 Concessions of the Province................................ 28
 1. Collection by the Lord Proprietary of Taxes regarded as unconstitutional... 28
  Port or Tonnage Duty.................................. 28
  Tobacco Tax.. 30
 2. Interference with the Colony's Right to Levy Taxes.......... 35
  Ordinary Licenses...................................... 35
  Tariff on Convicts..................................... 40
 3. Paper Money Controversy................................. 43
  Assembly displays its Ignorance of the Principles of Exchange 45
 4. Refusal of the Proprietary to share the Burdens of Taxation... 46
  Action of the Assembly on Supplies..................... 46
  Private Subscriptions................................... 47

Contents.

Assembly wins a Point.................................... 48
1756, a vote of £40,000................................. 49
The Land Tax.. 49
Taxation of Proprietary Estates......................... 50
Lord Baltimore's Indifference and Parsimony recoil upon him 52
Wisdom of Sharpe's Course, although he allows the Assembly to score another Point against the Proprietary......... 53

5. Pennsylvania's Influence upon Maryland................. 53
Land Tax in Pennsylvania; a Concession secured 54, 56
Maryland adopts Pennsylvania's Tactics.................... 56
Franklin's Influence..................................... 58
Pennsylvania's Victory over her Proprietaries............. 59

IV. CONCLUSION:

Dawn of Independence.................................... 60
Maryland's Indifference and "Unseasonable Parsimony" in the French and Indian War........................... 60
Crown Requisitions; Treatment of Roman Catholics 61, 64
Opposition to Proprietary Rule........................... 66
Where was the Assembly at fault?......................... 66
Explanations; the Proprietary at fault................... 67
Real Designs of the Assembly:
To limit Proprietary Authority........................ 68
To play into the Hands of the Crown................... 68
Indications of this:
Petitions to the Crown............................ 69
Calvert's Proposition to bribe the Assembly......... 69
Franklin's Second Mission (1764) to London.......... 72
No Desire for Union or Independence................. 72
Oppression of Great Britain; Stamp Act................... 73
Union a Necessity...................................... 73
Maryland's Opposition to Proprietary Rule a Preparation for the Struggle with the Crown, and finally Independence.... 73

MARYLAND'S ATTITUDE IN THE STRUGGLE FOR CANADA.

CHAPTER I.

INTRODUCTION.

The French and Indian War in America began in 1754 and continued until 1760, when Canada fell into the hands of the English. The French were successful for the first four years of the war, and the frontiers of Virginia, Maryland and Pennsylvania were at the mercy of the enemy during that time. The length of the struggle surprises one; certainly the English were stronger than the French in numbers and resources, and might have repelled the aggressions of the French in America by one or two decisive blows. It is true that England did not lend a helping hand in this colonial war until 1755, and at first sent out several inefficient commanders, but the chief cause of ill-fortune was the failure of the colonies to coöperate with one another and with Great Britain. While the colonies were organizing or trying to organize, the French were advancing under good leadership and encircling their opponents.

To a Marylander studying this period the following question suggests itself: How did my State behave? Certainly Maryland's welfare, indeed her very existence, was at stake; did she do her duty? These questions will be discussed in the following paper.

Maryland and Pennsylvania were the only colonies that remained under the Proprietary form of government down to the Revolution. Maryland's charter was a very liberal one; it gave large and extensive powers to the Proprietary, while at the same time it guaranteed the freemen of the province a voice in the laws by which they were to be governed; further, it contained one important and significant provision, namely, that no "imposition, custom or other taxation, rate, or contribution whatsoever" should be laid upon the province. Maryland was thus secured by the terms of her charter from an imposition of any kind on the part of Great Britain. Before the middle of the eighteenth century the colonies, particularly the Southern and Middle colonies, acted independently of each other in affairs of common concern, such as defense against the Indians. A union of all the colonies for their common defense had more than once been suggested, and efforts leading to that end were made from time to time. New England, for many reasons, physical and otherwise, was the first center of this movement, but the nearest approach to a general union was that suggested by the Albany convention of 1754. Indeed, down to this time the colonies had been unwilling to sacrifice any of their privileges for the sake of union, but with the progress of the war this feeling changed; as they saw their welfare threatened and their rights invaded, a sense of common interest impelled them to stand shoulder to shoulder in defending their territory. It proved a valuable lesson to them, for they received their training for the great conflict, so little anticipated, yet so soon to come. The Stamp Act cemented the confederation which the French and Indian War had begun.

The year 1751 marked the accession of Frederick, sixth Baron of Baltimore, as Lord Proprietary of Maryland. He was an unworthy scion of his ancestors, George and Cecilius Calvert. We find very few letters from Frederick among Gov. Sharpe's correspondence, and these are brief. He always appeared indifferent to the needs and welfare of his province, caring only for what he could get out of it, and his principal instructions to Sharpe were to see to the prompt collection of his revenue and to promote the interests of certain persons designated by him.¹

In 1753 Horatio Sharpe became Governor of Maryland, and continued in that office until 1769, occupying a position by no means enviable in these troublous times. The Governor was the intermediary between the Proprietary and the people. He was forced to obey the instructions of the Proprietor, and was usually regarded with undeserved dislike and suspicion by the Assembly for doing his duty. Sharpe steadily followed the difficult path of duty, however, better than most men in a like station. He was zealous in his efforts to carry out the instructions of the Crown, of the Proprietary, whose sworn deputy he was, and at the same time to appease the Assembly. Sharpe did all he could to arouse the Assembly to a sense of their danger, and engaged actively in raising troops and supplies for the service. He was constantly meditating on some expedient to overcome the obstinacy of the burgesses, sometimes suggesting that a poll-tax or stamp-tax be imposed, or that Parliament should take measures compelling the colonies to contribute their quotas. Sharpe even advanced from his own pocket bounty money which was used to enlist volunteers for frontier service. Subsequent history shows that his courage and fidelity to the trusts imposed on him were rightly respected.

The population of Maryland in 1756, as given by Sharpe in a report to the Lords of Trade, was 107,963 white and 46,225 black inhabitants, and of the former, Sharpe estimates that 26,000 were able to bear arms, all exemptions considered.² The militia of the province numbered 16,500, one-third of these being destitute of arms and the rest but poorly equipped. Another source of anxiety to Sharpe was his ill success in securing the passage of a good militia law by the Assembly, for the people were poorly armed, undisciplined, and could not be compelled to serve. As Sharpe said, there was nothing

---

¹ *Vide* Sharpe Cor. I. (Archives of Md.), 1753–1757, pp. 206, 127.

² Sharpe Correspondence, I., 353.

in Maryland deserving the name of fortification; Fort Cumberland was probably the nearest approach to it, but this was too far off in the wilderness to be of any great service. The military defenses of Maryland were in a very precarious state; she was fourth or fifth in strength among the colonies, but this strength was unorganized, and the territory of the province was, as said before, at the mercy of the enemy.

Let us look briefly at the attitude of the province toward its government. In the beginning the Proprietary was everything to the colony; but by successive steps the Assembly acquired privileges that belonged to the Lord Proprietor and made itself the real governing body of the province. Though large powers were given to the Lord Proprietor, the terms of the charter provided for the participation of the colonists in the legislative functions, the Crown having no direct supervision over the colony. To Lord Baltimore and his heirs, as Proprietors of Maryland, was granted the power to make laws for the province "by and with the advice, assent, and approbation of the said province, or the greatest part of them, or of their delegates or deputies." At first, the Lord Proprietary took the initiative in proposing legislation; the laws proposed were ratified or rejected at a mass-meeting of the freemen of the province. It was only a short time, however, till representative government developed. After 1638 the Provincial Assembly holds the initiative in legislation; to the Proprietary is left the veto power only. By an act passed at this session, provision was made for the election of delegates to the House of Burgesses, this body to consist of representatives elected by the freemen of each hundred, together with members of the Council, Lords of Manors, and any other "gentleman" summoned by special writ of the Proprietor.[1] In April, 1650, the Assembly met in two distinct branches; the Governor and his Council forming the Upper House, and the Burgesses the Lower House.[2] The Delegates, or Bur-

---

[1] *Maryland Archives, Assembly Proceedings, 1637-1664,* pp. 74, 75, 81, 82.
[2] *Ibid.,* p. 272.

gesses, were the elective representatives of the people; the Council, which formed the Upper House, represented the Lord Proprietor, and its members were summoned by special writs. They were the advisers of the executive, and at the same time formed one branch of the legislature. Frequent wrangling resulted between these two branches of the legislature, the one being the protector of the liberties of the people; the other, the conservative defenders of their lord's prerogatives. The popular branch continually gained ground at the expense of the prerogatives of the Lord Proprietary,[1] and by 1650 the Lower House had secured firm control of legislation in Maryland. This is evidenced by an act passed in that year, whereby it was enacted that "no Subsidies, ayde, Customes, taxes, or impositions shall hereafter bee layd assessed, leavyed or imposed upon the freemen of this Province or on theire Merchandize Goods or Chattles without the Consent and Approbation of the freemen of this Province their Deputies or the Major parte of them, first had and declared in a General Assembly of this Province."[2] In 1689 the Lord Proprietor lost his political rights in the province and Maryland became and remained a Crown colony till 1715. During this time Proprietary government lost much of its prestige, and the revenues which Lord Baltimore was still allowed to enjoy were attacked by the Assembly. Those of a public nature it desired to transfer to the Crown, to be used for the support of the province. The volume of legislation increases largely at this time, and we notice that laws were only made by the Assembly for short periods; old laws were continually repealed and reënacted; in this way the Assembly managed to keep a secure hold upon the government of the province. Besides they enacted against the Catholics severe laws, which gave offense to a large

---

[1] An act of 1638 declared that a General Assembly of "Freemen of the Province" should have "like power priveledges authority and Jurisdiction . . . as the house of Commons within the Realm of England" . . . Assembly Proceedings, 1638-1664, p. 75.

[2] Assembly Proceedings, 1650, p. 302.

element of the population. It is true this was the looked for result of Protestant ascendency and narrow-minded legislation; but it was opposed to the spirit of the Proprietary government, and rebuked the liberal policy of the Lords Proprietors.

By the time the Proprietary government was restored, in 1715, Maryland had almost learned to do without it; neither did its restoration give rise to any marked joy or loyalty on the part of the people, nor did it regain its former political status. From now until the French and Indian War we note the increasing dissensions between the Assembly and the Proprietary; many of the privileges of the latter were gradually and imperceptibly slipping away. In 1739, during Governor Ogle's administration, an attack was begun upon the revenues of the Proprietary, and was only concluded by the overthrow of the Proprietary government itself. This leads us to an explanation of the causes that underlay the conduct of Maryland during that war. The Lower House had become the mainspring of the provincial government; it assumed the protection of the liberties of its constituents, endeavored to make laws for the people and not for the Proprietor, and not only defended their rights and privileges from any encroachment by the Proprietary, but in turn encroached upon the prerogatives of that government. The Assembly now saw and decided to take advantage of a favorable opportunity to wrest from Proprietary rule in Maryland the last vestiges of its power.

CHAPTER II.

FRENCH AND INDIAN WAR.

That the events which follow may be clearly understood, it will be advisable, first, to give a brief sketch of the early period of the French and Indian War, pointing out the part played by Maryland.

The French and Indian War was a struggle between two great nations for the possession of the North American Continent. Every colony was deeply concerned in the issue of the contest. The French were the first to explore the Mississippi valley, several expeditions being made in the latter part of the seventeenth century. The claims of the English, of course, were based on the discoveries of the Cabots, Raleigh, Gilbert and others, and the colonial charters vaguely describe the grants to the colonies as extending westward to the "South Sea" or extending between two parallels of latitude "from sea to sea."[1] The old grudges between France and England were thus carried to America, and the most hostile feelings existed between the two all through the eighteenth century, especially from the peace of Utrecht, 1713. Toward the middle of the century each of the two nations made haste to occupy as much territory as possible. A collision could not long be avoided. The French asserted their sovereignty to the territory west of the Alleghanies, and strove to carry out the gigantic scheme of connecting Canada and the great lakes with Louisiana and the Gulf of Mexico by a cordon of fortified posts for the purpose of hemming in the English colonies and preventing their expansion toward the west. It was their steady advance in realizing this idea that so terrified the colonists.

---

[1] Charters of Va. and Mass. Dinwiddie Papers, Vol. I., 381.

The conflict was precipitated by the formation of the Ohio Company (1748), which was organized by a party of Virginians; to them was given a grant of 500,000 acres on the Ohio river, chiefly to the north of it and between the Monongahela and Kanawha. Their purpose was trade with the Indians, and in return for the privileges given them they agreed to induce migration thither and build a fort to protect the settlement. The French took active steps to repel this advance of the English into disputed territory, and occupied the Ohio valley with their forces at once. As this was a direct attack upon Virginia land, Gov. Dinwiddie made preparations to oppose it, and duly informed the Lords of Trade of their encroachments, their apparent designs, and the alarm that existed among the colonists. Some supplies were sent him, and at the same time it was suggested that the various Assemblies of the colonies should send representatives to a common meeting-place for the purpose of making a treaty with the Six Nations[1] and providing measures for defense. Gov. Sharpe of Maryland received a letter[2] from Lord Holdernesse, Secretary of State, warning him of the approaching hostilities of the French and Indians on the western frontier, urging him to be on the alert, to put himself in close communication with other Governors, and when occasion demanded it, to convene his Assembly and to bring before it the necessity of mutual assistance and coöperation. The same communication was sent to all the provincial governors, and from this time on Maryland was constantly appealed to by Virginia and the British government. In October, 1753, Gov. Dinwiddie sent Major George Washington to the commander of the French forces on the Ohio, " to know his reasons for his invading His Majesty of Great Britain's Dominions."[3] The mission of Washington proved unsuccessful, and Gov. Dinwiddie then began active prepar-

---

[1] The famous Indian Confederacy of Western New York.
[2] Sharpe Correspondence, I., 3, 4.
[3] Ibid., I., 10. Dinwiddie Papers, I., 49, note.

ations for defense. In this, however, he met with considerable opposition from his own Assembly, and secured a vote of supplies with difficulty. He was much embarrassed in his plans, and as the exigencies of the times called for coöperation on the part of the governors of the colonies, he sent letters to them, in which he recounted the results of Washington's mission, the strength and designs of the French, and asked immediate aid.[1] In April, 1754, hostilities began with the capture by the French of an English fort which Gov. Dinwiddie had ordered to be built at the junction of the Alleghany and Monongahela rivers, and which the conquerors strengthened considerably and named Fort Duquesne, after the Governor of Canada.[2] Dinwiddie's energies were fruitless for the time, and he complained bitterly of the lack of help; in a letter to James Abercromby, agent of Virginia at London, after passing a compliment upon the behavior of North Carolina, he writes,—" Maryland and Pennsylvania, two Proprietary governments, do nothing, though equally concerned and more exposed than this dominion. . . . This is an affair of the greatest consequence to the Nation and the Colonies on this Continent."[3] In the meantime, a body of Virginia militia, with Washington second in command, had been sent by Gov. Dinwiddie to protest against the proceedings of the French commander, Contrecœur, and on the march learned that the fort had been taken. Washington defeated a party of French under de Jumonville in a preliminary skirmish; but a large force were now advancing from Fort Duquesne to attack the English, and Washington, who had succeeded to the chief command, fell back to Great Meadows, on a branch of the Youghiogeny, where he awaited the enemy. Here he hastily erected rude defenses, and gave them, from the nature of the occasion, the name of Fort Necessity. Washington, however, was unable to with-

---

[1] Dinwiddie Papers, I., 61-73.
[2] Fully treated in Sharpe Correspondence, I., 197.
[3] Dinwiddie Papers, I., 211.

stand the superior numbers of the French, and therefore surrendered (July 3, 1754). This he did upon honorable terms and returned to Virginia.[1]

Meantime, in accordance with the suggestions of the Board of Trade, a general convention was held at Albany, June 19, 1754, and commissioners were present from seven colonies. Maryland was among this number, but it was with difficulty that Sharpe prevailed on the Assembly to provide for the commissioners appointed by the Governor and to vote a purse of £500 as a present to the Six Indian Nations, and in reference to his proposition that they aid Virginia Sharpe writes: "So insuperably indifferent or perverse were they that all they consulted was how to save appearances and seem to be disposed to encourage that important enterprise."[2] The purposes of the convention were, first, to make a treaty with the Six Nations; and secondly, to form a plan of concerted action among the colonies to drive away the French. The Indians were appeased with presents. The second object was then taken up and debated, and a union of all the colonies was declared necessary. A plan, devised by Franklin, was proposed and adopted.[3] This plan, however, provided for a perpetual union, which was certainly premature, and Maryland for one was not prepared to favor it; in consequence, her Assembly rejected it by the unanimous vote of its members. Nevertheless, this step toward uniting the colonies into one government was very significant, for it was the forerunner of confederation. The Albany congress made no preparations for defense, but decided to await the action of Parliament upon the scheme for union which had been proposed. The surrender of Washington, July 3, 1754, caused considerable alarm to the Southern provinces, and the gov-

---

[1] For terms of the capitulation of Washington *vide* Sharpe Cor. I., 78-79 (extract from Calvert Papers).

[2] Sharpe Correspondence, I., 69.

[3] Franklin's plan and comments: *vide* II. W. Preston, "Documents illustrative of American History," pp. 170-187.

ernors bestirred themselves to raise men and supplies. Gov. Dinwiddie again complains: "What a poor situation am I in, in executing the commands of his majesty; no assistance from the neighboring colonies; Maryland and Pennsylvania so obstinate as not to grant any supplies whatever."[1] He said that Virginia was not able to bear the burden of the war alone, and had already suggested on June 18, 1754, that Parliament compel each colony to raise a proportionate quota of the general fund. This proposition was repeatedly made by him to the Secretary of State and Board of Trade. He writes: "The intolerable obstinacy of our neighboring colonies and their disobedience to His Majesty's commands is not to be paralleled in history; if they had entered heartily into the affair, I am assured the French at this day would have been drove off the Ohio, and I am of (the) opinion, nothing will bring them to their duty but a general Poll Tax of 2s. 6d. sterling, by a British Act of Parliament."[2] However, Maryland, whose frontier was exposed to the enemy, with no defenses to hinder their advance, was sufficiently aroused to a sense of her danger to vote (February 25, 1754) a supply of £6000, to be appropriated to the aid of Virginia; but this grant was conditional upon the yielding of certain concessions by the Proprietary government. The Maryland Assembly was still as "obstinate" as ever.

The English government, aroused by the imminence of the danger, made preparations to take an active part in the campaign. They deemed it necessary to send out a general officer to take command, for it was thought that Sharpe and the other colonial governors would have all they could do to enlist men and secure funds from their Assemblies. A land expedition against Fort Duquesne and a naval expedition in North American waters were determined upon; and General Edward Braddock was ordered to America with two regiments to take command of the land forces in America.

In the meantime, Governor Sharpe, who had had military

---

[1] Dinwiddie Papers, I., 253. [2] *Ibid.*, I., 254.

experience, was appointed to the chief command, with the rank of lieutenant-colonel, for Maryland was looked upon as a good center from which to operate against the French.[1] He was in a state of constant anxiety, but did his best to raise forces and obtain supplies with which to carry out his instructions as commander-in-chief. But Sharpe by no means received the encouragement he had hoped, and therefore could not expect to execute his commission "with any great eclat"; "I wish I may be able to do it," he says, "with some small reputation."[2] His appointment, however, was only a temporary one, and he was superseded by Braddock upon the latter's arrival on February 20, 1755. The reception General Braddock met was far from encouraging.

Sharpe brooded constantly upon some remedy for the perverseness of colonial Assemblies. He echoed the views of Governor Dinwiddie and others as to the proper method of securing the coöperation of the colonies, and suggested to Cecilius Calvert, uncle and secretary of Frederick, Lord Baltimore, September 15, 1754, that if it were thought proper to bring in a bill in Parliament to compel the colonial governments to contribute their quotas, one of the following ways might be proposed to raise the funds: 1. By imposing a poll tax; or, 2. By a duty on the importation of spirituous liquors; or, 3. By a stamp duty—on deeds and writings. "These hints," he says, "I have taken the liberty to submit to you in case the British Legislature should think proper to interfere in this American contention more than it has hitherto done."[3] This gives evidence of the extremities to which the governors were driven, but radical measures were not attempted by England, and indeed it is doubtful if they could have been enforced. Governor Sharpe lived to see his suggestion tried and fail. The English government resorted to the more prudent but less imperative method of Crown requisitions. It was expected

---

[1] Sharpe's commission, *vide* Sharpe Cor. I., 73-74 (July, 1754).
[2] Sharpe Correspondence, I., 110.   [3] *Ibid.*, I., 99.

that the raising, subsisting and quartering of troops raised in a province should be provided for by that province, but that affairs of more general concern should be paid for out of a "common fund,"[1] to be established for the benefit of all the colonies, collectively, in North America. And it seems to have been the intention of Great Britain to form a plan for the general union of the colonies for defense, for it was mentioned in a letter from Sir Thomas Robinson, Secretary of State, to Gov. Sharpe,[2] and Gov. Morris, of Pennsylvania, wrote[3] to Sharpe that he had received hints from England that a plan of union for military purposes was under the consideration of the ministry. No such measures were put into effect, however; union could not be forced upon the colonies in accord with the dictates of Parliament,—it had to come from within.

During this period of their history the lack of unity among the colonies in facing a danger which menaced them all alike was very marked; but in one thing there seemed to be considerable unity, and that was the almost universal resistance which the colonial Assemblies offered to their governors when attempting to carry out their instructions. We see this even among the New England colonies, but especially south of New York, so that Gov. Sharpe, in the autumn of 1754, said that by this time he had learned "not to entertain very sanguine hopes of the resolutions of American Assemblies."[4] Their professions of regard for his Majesty's interests were loyal enough, and supply bills were freely presented; but the fact is, all the Assemblies looked upon this as a good opportunity to establish the liberties of the commonwealths on a firmer basis, and hence, when voting supplies, they attached to their bills objectionable clauses, sought to wrest important concessions from their rulers, and gain

---

[1] Sharpe Correspondence, I., 108.
[2] October 26, 1754.
[3] December 3, 1754.
[4] Sharpe Correspondence, I., 109.

for themselves complete self-government. Of course, these objectionable bills the governors were obliged to veto in the interest of their proprietors, or the English government itself; and Sharpe complained that they "endeavored to cast an odium on their respective governors by laying them under the necessity of rejecting such bills as were presented them."

However, when the alarm in the Ohio Valley became more general and the war assumed greater proportions, New England came forward and contributed her share; New York lent liberal aid; New Jersey seemed to partake of the infection that possessed Pennsylvania and refused to do anything; "they seem to have had nothing else in view at their meetings," says Sharpe, "but to show the greatest disregard of and contempt for the old gentleman's recommendations"[1] (referring to Gov. Belcher). Virginia had contributed £10,000 and soon afterward £20,000 more, and Maryland had contributed £6000 besides the £500 given to the Six Nations.

Maryland had constantly before her the example of her sister Proprietary colony, Pennsylvania;[2] Sharpe was continually expressing fears that the obstinacy of the Pennsylvania Assembly would have an influence upon that of Maryland, and subsequent events prove that the latter was inclined to be subservient to the policy maintained by the former. The terror of the inhabitants on the western frontier was very great; the Indians made many incursions upon Maryland and Virginia soil, killing a number of families and destroying their property. This occasioned great alarm and many of the people in the western part of the province abandoned their homes; such was the state of affairs until the arrival of Braddock raised their hopes. Fort Cumberland was the only protection which the western inhabitants had, and this was inadequate; small forces only could be raised for the defense of

---

[1] Sharpe Correspondence, I., 110.
[2] Pennsylvania's influence on Maryland, see below, ch. III., sec. 5.

the frontier. On April 14, 1755, General Braddock met the colonial governors [1] at Alexandria, and a plan of operations was agreed upon, Braddock hoping to enlist the active sympathies of the colonies. In this, however, he was to be disappointed. The Assembly of Maryland was again called to vote a supply, but Sharpe was able to do nothing with them. The deaths of twenty-six of the "distant inhabitants," as a result of the encroachments and devastations of the French and their savage allies, had no effect upon the Assembly, for they "set nothing in competition with the points for which they were contending," and, says Gov. Sharpe, "the lives and safeties of the people must submit to their caprice and humour." He was obliged to prorogue the Assembly until the following year, for they refused to do anything, except upon their own conditions. Braddock was much incensed at the cold reception which he received from the provincial Assemblies, and was highly displeased that no common fund was provided for his disposal in prosecuting the war. He communicated with the governors, Sharpe among the number, stating his expectations and the quota which each should furnish. Sharpe again proposed a poll tax, and urged, besides, that the power to levy the tax be taken from the Legislature and put in the hands of the several Governors and Councils, in order to "prevent useless disputes and controversies."[2] Sharpe, in his anxiety to obey instructions, called a meeting of his Assembly for June 23, 1755, but with no sanguine feelings; he looked forward to a series of disputes, and thought that rather than aid Braddock they would indulge in fault-finding because his troops had carried off servants, carriages and horses belonging to the inhabitants over whose lands they had marched.

The Assembly offered £5000, but the measures proposed for raising the loan were such as the Governor could not sanction. Sharpe was much disconcerted and distressed to see

---
[1] Governors of Va., Md., Penn., N. Y., and Mass.
[2] Sharpe Correspondence, I., 203.

the condition of the people on the western frontier without being able to help them. He was led to say, "the Assembly will never recede from the points that his Lordship's instructions oblige me to insist on tho' half the province should be depopulated."[1] He even thought, should Braddock have "taken the French Forts on the Ohio," he could not hold them, for the colonies would not support a garrison or supply it there "without compulsion."

The Braddock expedition against Fort Duquesne, as is well known, ended in complete failure :[2] suffice it to say that the failure, which was due to the lack of effective coöperation on the part of the colonies coupled with Braddock's own lack of good judgment, gave the French an alarming advantage, for it was followed by the disgraceful retreat to Philadelphia of Col. Dunbar,[3] who commanded the forces after the death of Braddock, and the abandonment of the field; this left the frontier without defense, except such as a hundred or two half-starved provincial troops could give. All the barriers were thrown down, and Sharpe thought that 2000 regular troops with as many Indians could have marched to the Chesapeake almost without hindrance; for such was the opinion he had of the 18,000 Maryland militia and the Virginia troops. If the French had taken full advantage of their victory they might have made the invasion of Maryland an entering wedge and thus have cut the colonies in two, as the British afterwards attempted to do during the Revolution. However, this was not done, for efforts were now being made to oppose the French in the north; and the latter, seeing that the real struggle would be in Canada and on the lakes, withdrew a large portion of their forces from the Ohio. But much injury was committed and some blood shed on the defenseless frontier; the western inhabitants were terrified and fled to the more populous sections of the province.

---

[1] Sharpe Cor. I., 239.
[2] Orme's account of Braddock's defeat, July 9, 1755; Sharpe Cor. I., 252.
[3] Dinwiddie Papers, II., 139.

Governor Sharpe did what he could to stop this flight and persuade the people to return to their homes. Fort Cumberland was garrisoned by provincial troops, and several small palisade forts were constructed and occupied by volunteers; these served as places of refuge for the panic-stricken people. The cost of these defenses was defrayed by private subscriptions contributed by the Council and people.

Down to February, 1756, all that was contributed toward the campaign was £6000 and a small force of troops. New York and Pennsylvania did better than this, although the latter, considering her danger, was also slow to act. New Jersey did as well. Virginia, though at first more directly affected, contributed nearly £100,000 and a larger force of men in the same time. Even South Carolina was not more backward than Maryland. This was so despite the fact that the latter province was looked upon as the center of action; her own governor, in consequence, being appointed commander-in-chief temporarily.

Sharpe was powerless to control events. However, a small company of sixty men under Captain Dagworthy was raised to accompany Braddock. Maryland had no effective militia law, and the Assembly could not be prevailed on to pass one, so that the difficulty in raising and disciplining troops was next to that of securing a vote of supplies. Gov. Sharpe estimated that the three colonies, Maryland, Virginia and Pennsylvania, alone could furnish 80,000 men, but it was with the greatest difficulty that a few hundred could be pressed into service and supported.

After Braddock's failure, the conquest of Fort Duquesne was left to the southern colonies, and Sharpe was constantly importuned to attack it, but never secured support enough to risk the attempt. Nothing was done against the fort until 1758. Gov. Shirley, of Massachusetts, was appointed commander-in-chief of the American forces to succeed Braddock, and this was an indication that the war against the French would be fought out largely by New England.

Though nothing aggressive was done south of New York, nevertheless Gov. Sharpe did not cease his efforts to secure a handsome appropriation from his Assembly for the purpose of defending the frontier and aiding Shirley in the north. The exposure of the western inhabitants to French and Indian raids occasioned constant alarm, and the pressure brought upon the Assembly was very great. Something had to be done at once. The Assembly yielded; at the next session (February 23, 1756), a vote of £40,000 was passed. But Sharpe was still much discouraged, for he said his experience had taught him that there was a " wide difference between voting a sum of money and granting or raising it." The money was raised, however, and used for defense, but we shall find that in this case it was the Proprietary and not the Assembly that had yielded.

CHAPTER III.

"BONES OF CONTENTION."

THE ASSEMBLY vs. THE LORD PROPRIETARY.

A Marylander can feel little pride, nay, rather humiliation for the conduct of his State during this period of her history. Upon whom rests the responsibility for this attitude of Maryland at such a time? Upon the Proprietary? upon the Province? or upon both? To find an explanation of the backwardness of the Province, let us examine the points at issue between the people and the Proprietary government. They were as follows:

1. The collection of revenues by the Proprietary which were regarded as illegal; for instance, the port or tonnage duty and the tobacco tax.

2. Interference with the colony's right to levy taxes and control public revenues; for example, the contest about the tax on ordinary licenses and the duty on imported convicts.

3. The paper-money controversy.

4. Refusal of the Proprietary to share with the Province the burdens of the war and waive his right to the exemption of his estates from taxation.

5. The example of her sister colony, Pennsylvania.

The revenues[1] enjoyed by the Proprietor fall into two classes: first, those which arose from his ownership of the soil, vested in him by the charter, or so-called "territorial rights." They were: 1. Quit rents, or small fixed charges received by the Proprietary from lands subgranted by him. 2. Caution money, a revenue that arose from a new system, adopted in 1683, whereby any person could sue out a war-

---

[1] Kilty, "Landholder's Assistant," pp. 254-268.

rant for land upon the payment of a certain sum, called "caution money." 3. Alienation fines (including fines upon devises), sums paid to the Proprietary for the privilege of conveying land from one person to another. These were private rights of his lordship.

Secondly, those which rested upon the bounty of the people and were granted to him in his sovereign capacity as ruler of the Province, or so-called "rights of jurisdiction." They were: 1. The port or tonnage duty. 2. The tobacco duty. 3. Fines and forfeitures. 4. Duty on ordinary licenses; hawkers' and peddlers' licenses and a few others of no special importance. These were the public revenues of the Proprietor. While both these classes of revenue were sanctioned by the charter, there was still a wide distinction between the two. When, in 1689, the Proprietary government lost its authority, the Proprietor also lost, for the time, most of his public revenues but he retained his private revenues as landlord of the soil.

1.—COLLECTION BY THE LORD PROPRIETARY OF TAXES THAT WERE REGARDED AS UNCONSTITUTIONAL.

The public revenues of the Proprietor were constant "bones of contention" between the Assembly and Lord Baltimore; it was these that caused most of the disputes that arrested the coöperation of Maryland in the French and Indian War. Although the port or tonnage duty originated in 1646, it was first permanently levied by the Act of 1661 entitled "An Act for Porte dutyes and Masters of Ships."[1] It was enacted that . . . . "all vessels not belonging to the province, having a deck flush fore and aft, coming in and trading within the Province should pay for Port Duties or Anchorage half a pound of powder and three pounds of shot or so much in value for every ton of burden to the Lord Proprietor and his heirs." . . . But it was afterward com-

---

[1] Assembly Proceedings, 1661, p. 418.

muted to fourteen pence per ton, and this revenue was enjoyed by the Proprietor unmolested until 1692. At this time, Maryland being under Royal government, the port duty was claimed by the Assembly as a public revenue. The Assembly urged the ingenious but false argument that the revenue was a fort duty and not a port duty; that though the journals of the Assembly and the original act itself had been lost or made away with, yet after a thorough examination into the reasons for making the law, they had found it "was for building of Forts and finding of powder and shott for the Country's use .... and the duty was always called by the inhabitants 'Fort Duetys and not Port Duetyes.'" The revenue amounted then to eight hundred pounds sterling annually, and it seemed to distress the Assembly greatly that the King should be burdened with the building of forts for the Province while the Lord Proprietor was allowed to enjoy this large revenue.

The attempt to show that this revenue was a fort duty and not a port duty, if successful, would have classed it among other revenues granted for defense which were repealed by the general repealing act of 1704. The Proprietor's agents collected this revenue in peace until 1739, when the old sores broke out afresh and became more virulent than ever. A systematic attack upon the Proprietary revenues was then begun and continued down to the Revolution. The port duty proved a constant grievance, for the Assembly pronounced it contrary to the reason and institution of the duty in the act of 1661, and took the ground "that all taxes not imposed or at least sanctioned by themselves were illegal." The Assembly held that the duty had been repealed by the general repealing act of 1704. But legally the Assembly's case was a weak one; the Crown did not assent to a repeal of the port duty in 1704. Moreover, the Assembly really recognized the legality of the port duty, for when, in 1733, provision was made for a redemption fund in the Paper Currency Act, the appropriation of this revenue for such a purpose was specially exempted.

Though a duty on exported tobacco was levied in Maryland as early as 1638, it was the act of 1671 that occasioned so much dispute subsequently. It was entitled an "Act for the Rayseing and Provideing a Support for his Lordship . . . dureing his natureall life . . . and towards the defraying the Public Charges of Government."[1] By this act the sum of two shillings sterling was imposed as a duty upon every hogshead of tobacco which should be shipped "in any Ship or vessell" out of the province, but it was specially provided that one-half of the revenue thereby raised should be used for the constant maintenance of a magazine with arms and ammunition for the defense of the province and other public charges. A concluding clause directed that this act should continue during the natural life of Cecilius, then Lord Baltimore, and "for one Cropp more next after his decease and noe longer." It was also agreed that the Proprietor should receive his rents and fines for the alienation of lands in good tobacco, when tendered, at the rate of two pence per pound. However, by subsequent acts, the act of 1671 was continued during the lives of his successors, Charles Calvert and Benedict Leonard Calvert. When the government was seized by the Crown in 1691, the tobacco tax of two shillings was collected and lodged in the public treasury, and when the first royal governor, Copley, entered upon his office (1692), the Assembly settled upon him one shilling, or one-half the duty which had been appropriated by former acts for the support and defense of the province. Lord Baltimore had always claimed the other half, as of the nature of a private contract between himself and his tenants, in consideration for the loss he sustained by receiving his quit-rents in tobacco at the rate of two pence per pound. Receiving no benefit therefrom, his agent, Henry Darnall, petitioned the Assembly for the privilege of collecting this and other of his lordship's revenues. The Assembly replied evasively, but the King approved his claim and he continued to enjoy the twelve

---

[1] Assembly Proceedings, Vol. II. (1666-1676), pp. 284-286.

pence tariff. On Sept. 19, 1715, it was raised to eighteen pence per hogshead, and in 1716 this revenue was further increased, the Assembly purchasing the quit-rents and fines outright for a duty of two shillings per hogshead and an additional fifteen pence, twelve pence being for the support of the Governor, and three pence for arms and ammunition. These provisions were continued by an act of 1717, and were allowed to expire in 1733. Lord Baltimore thereupon, under color of the act of 1704, resumed the collection of his quit-rents and twelve pence per hogshead for the support of the government, which in the interval seems not to have been collected. It was continued without opposition until 1739, when trouble began, and the Assembly of 1739 spent a large portion of its session in discussing the legality of the tobacco tax. "During that period, 1733–1739, the Act of 1704 was looked on as a Law in Force and Being," says Governor Ogle, "until some Gentlemen of new Light (for I find we have new Light in Politicks as well as in Religion) lately undertook to undeceive us in this particular." The action of the Proprietor in collecting this twelve pence was denounced as illegal and unwarranted, and the Assembly took the untenable ground "that Acts passed during the period of Royal Government were not meant to extend to his Lordship, that the revenue had not been properly applied by the Proprietary, that the Law of 1704 was a 'mixed consideration,' dependent upon the proviso that Lord Baltimore receive his quit-rents and fines in tobacco." . . . The Lower House adopts this report of its Committee on Grievances, insisting that they, as British subjects, " wish to maintain to themselves and their constituents the liberty . . . of not being liable to the payment of any money, Tax, Impost or Duty, except such as are raised . . . by themselves." To give evidence of their good faith, the Assembly passed a bill giving twelve pence per hogshead to the Governor for his support. This was an equivalent of the twelve pence of the act of 1704, the collection of which by the Proprietary officers was declared illegal. The Upper House rejected the bill. Gov. Ogle tried to persuade the Assembly that they were in error, but they were not to be persuaded. The Lower House was not satisfied to let the matter rest here, and passed a bill for the appointment of an agent in London to lay their grievances before Lord Baltimore, and if he should fail to adjust them, to bring them before the King in Council. As the Lower House reserved to itself exclusive control of the agents both as to appointment and payment, the Upper House rejected the measure with the comment,—"A prettier Scheme for Power and Profit, in our little World of Politicks, can hardly be thought of." The Lower House argues ominously : " The people of Maryland think the Proprietary takes Money from them unlawfully, the Proprietary says he has a right to . . . his Majesty must determine and we must have a suitable agent in London to act for the people. . . . The people of Maryland have spirit enough and we hope will find means without this Bill to do themselves Justice."

After opening this broadside upon the Proprietary, Maryland kept up the fight without intermission until she became an independent State. The entire session of the Assembly of 1739 was given up to constant quarrels and bickerings between the representatives of the people and the partisans of the Proprietor, the Governor assuming the role of peacemaker. As a result, we find no new laws on the statute-books in 1739 and 1740.

The Lower House was not to be frustrated in its efforts to secure an agent in London, and their persistence was rewarded with success. In 1740 a colonial agent was retained, and two addresses were prepared stating their grievances, one to the Proprietor, the other to the King, the latter to be presented only in case the former failed of its object. The address to the Proprietor was presented and its response was submitted to the Assembly in 1744. It was conciliatory in tone and contained thanks for the evidences of good will manifested by the colonists toward his Majesty's government, but beyond mere empty promises and polite expressions it availed nothing toward the settling of the controversy. These differences with the Proprietary gave rise to a political faction which continued through the remaining days of the colonial period. At regular intervals down to 1771 resolutions were passed directed against the tonnage and tobacco duties, and the antagonism of this faction increased as the outbreak of war occasioned new demands for revenue. It was held that the law of 1704 was a perpetual one; it was denied that laws made for his Majesty's government would not hold under Proprietary government, for the province continued to be "the Kings Government." The "mixed consideration" was also denied to be a necessary part of the act, and the Assembly was scored because it had made no objection to the collection of the tax until 1739. "The Right of the Act of 1704," says Calvert, "is so undeniable Apparent with the Crown and with Lord Baltimore as his Majesty's Hereditary Governor of Maryland, Its Quality is unto a Diamond not to be altered but by its own Power." . . . But Calvert struck at the seat of the dispute when he hinted that "the present legislators do not possess the same kindly spirit toward the administration that their ancestors did." In justice to the Proprietary be it said there is no evidence among the laws of Maryland of a repeal of the act of 1704. The popular branch of the Assembly were clearly at fault in the view they took. It was the attempt of a political faction in the province to wrest from Lord Baltimore privileges that were properly his. There had grown up a strong party opposed to the government in everything, and if there had been no check upon their designs, or had the Lord Proprietary not been as liberal as he was, he might have been stripped of all his political rights ere this. As it was, Baltimore may have made a mistake in failing to make concessions which would have led to an adjustment of the difficulties between him and the people. The Assembly was unfortunate in having to deal at this time with a Proprietor who, unlike his predecessors, cared little for his province and was of no benefit to it at all. Frederick was satisfied with Sharpe's administration so long as he kept his income intact, but was unwilling to tolerate any petitions from the Assembly. The collection of the tobacco and tonnage duties remained ever afterward a standing complaint, and was often an excuse for a dispute or a delay in legislation throughout Sharpe's entire term. Frequent attempts were made to mortgage this revenue when appropriating a supply, but in every case the bill was vetoed by the Upper House.

In 1756 another effort was made to secure an agent in London to bring their troubles before the King in Council, and a paper was circulated among the people to raise subscriptions for the purpose. They had come to the belief that the duties were illegal and were very much wrought up. Sharpe appreciated the situation; he confessed he thought the people unreasonable in their views, but urged Baltimore to allow the dispute to be brought before the Privy Council or be submitted for an opinion to the Attorney-General. Sharpe felt that if Frederick would but submit to a hearing he would be sustained, the people would be satisfied with the result and further controversy prevented. But Sharpe's advice was not heeded, and Lord Baltimore peremptorily forbade him from hearing any proposal by the Assembly concerning the appointment of an agent. Sure enough, as Sharpe had said, Frederick's resistance confirmed many people in the opinion that the money was collected without the sanction of the law. However, payment was not resisted and the taxes were collected as long as Proprietary rule lasted, subject, though, to periodic condemnation.

According to the Governor's estimate in 1756, the port duty yielded then a revenue of £800 or £900 annually; the tobacco duty, £1400, most of which was the annual salary of the Lieutenant-Governor, the rest being paid to the Proprietor.

2.—INTERFERENCE WITH THE COLONY'S RIGHT TO LEVY TAXES.

Ordinary Licenses.—The ordinary licenses were revenues that arose from annual fees exacted from the innkeepers of the province. They were first levied in "An Acte Regulateing Ordinaryes and Limitting the number of them within this Province," passed by the Assembly in 1678. By the terms of this act a license fee of 2000 pounds of tobacco was imposed upon every ordinary keeper who kept an inn within two miles of the " City of St. Maryes," or 1200 pounds for a similar privilege in any county.[1] This was an annual fee and yielded a goodly revenue to Lord Baltimore, to whom it was granted.[2] It appears that the Lord Proprietor's secretary received the ordinary license fees from 1678 until 1692. They were given him by his lordship in lieu of certain clearance fees which had become more lucrative and therefore made the exchange desirable. This was public revenue, and in that eventful year, 1692, the Assembly, upon the plea that the Secretary only enjoyed it through his lordship's bounty, and that his lord was no longer in authority, transferred the ordinary license fund to the royal governor. Upon this, the Secretary appealed to the King and complained of the confiscation, which caused him a yearly loss of £150.[3] In consequence, the King in Council disallowed this act of the Assembly, and the license fees were restored to the Secretary. Thus the Proprietor gained another point which was won through the aid of the Crown. Ordinary licenses were continued by various acts till 1729.[4] In 1735,[5] another "act for regulating Innholders and Ordinary keepers " was passed,

---

[1] The penalty for an attempt to keep without a license was a forfeiture of 10,000 pounds of tobacco.

[2] Or rather was taken by him, as his by prerogative. Sharpe Correspondence, I., 235.

[3] Council Proceedings (Md. Archives), 1692, pp. 386, 438, 451, 456.

[4] Bacon's Laws of Maryland, 1717, ch. 1 ; 1726, ch. 10.

[5] Bacon's Laws of Maryland, 1735, ch. 8.

which expired in 1740. The Assembly of 1739 had refused to renew this revenue to the Proprietor, and in 1740 the ordinary licenses were appropriated by law, with the consent of the Proprietor, to defray the expense of raising men for the Carthagena expedition, and in 1746 to help an intended expedition against Canada. In that way the ordinary license fees were mortgaged until 1754.

By an act of 1735, hawkers, peddlers and petty chapmen were required to take out a license annually. This also yielded a fee of £5 for each license, which was given to the Proprietor for the support of the government. The act expired in 1740.

Maryland, until 1753, had never been directly threatened by a French invasion. Although war had been carried on with the French for half a century, the Canada border was always the scene of action. The people of Maryland had consequently taken no part in this warfare, save by an occasional contribution. Even the purse of £500 to be presented to the Six Nations at the Albany Congress was not secured from the Assembly without considerable wrangling between the two houses, for the Lower Branch wished to replace the money taken out of the Loan Office by "License Money and Fines and Forfeitures" arising from other sources. The Upper House resisted this invasion of Lord Baltimore's privileges. The dispute was finally settled by a resolution of the House of Delegates "to take £500 current money out of the Treasurer's hand" to purchase presents for the Indians. Increased pressure and persuasion soon brought the Assembly to a sense of their duty, and in May, 1754, an act was passed by the Lower House to appropriate £3000 in aid of Virginia, but it never became law; for among the ways and means reported by the committee for raising the fund, an additional tax of £1 was placed on ordinary licenses, and a £3 annual license on hawkers and peddlers; likewise additional taxes upon indented servants and imported negroes. No objection was made to the latter, but the license fees killed the bill. A conference of the two houses led to an adjustment of the dispute, and the Assembly was prorogued until July. Sharpe, on becoming Lieutenant-Governor of the Province, had received private instructions from Lord Baltimore to order the Proprietary agent to receive the revenue arising from ordinary licenses, but he answered that it was impossible, for the license fees were already taxed to pay off a loan made in 1746 and this had not been fully redeemed. Frederick wished to see no retrenchment of the Proprietary revenue, while the Assembly was determined he should share their burdens. The Proprietor had not received the license fees since 1739, and his only title to them previous to that time was the will of the Assembly. It was the prompting of an indifferent and selfish spirit that now led him to interfere and prevent the province from appropriating this revenue for the public good. Ordinary licenses were not a permanent fund voted to the use of the Proprietor and his heirs. The purpose of the Assembly in imposing these licenses was the "better regulating of ordinary-keepers and limiting their number within the province." And to that end a tax had been placed which served incidentally as a source of revenue. It was granted to Lord Baltimore only, however, for temporary periods; these grants were subject to renewal, and were accepted as gifts by the Proprietor till 1739, when the Assembly refused to continue them longer. Now that the Province needed public money, it proposed to claim its own and avoid the burden of an increase of taxation. Frederick's claim to this fund rested upon precedent alone, and even had it been stronger, he should have waived it in this time of public danger. His selfishness aggravated the tardiness of Maryland in responding to the appeals of her sister, Virginia, and the instructions of the English government. Sharpe, Frederick's own appointee, held these views, though he never expressed himself in language quite so strong. The provincial Assembly had long before entered into a contest with its Proprietary for supremacy, and now that an opportunity offered, with the Proprietary government at its weakest stage, they meant to settle it in their own favor. Thus matters stood; and the government was practically at a standstill when the people of Maryland received the news of Washington's surrender at Fort Necessity. The Assembly at this critical moment at once surprised and exasperated Didwiddie and the ministry; Sharpe it irritated, but did not surprise, for he knew his men. Upon the defeat of Washington, Sharpe called a special session for the consideration of a supply. He addressed the Assembly in these words: "In This Emergency the Hopes and Expectations of our Neighbors whom in Duty, Honour and Interest we are Engaged to Support and Defend are fixed upon us for assistance; and What must the World think of our Conduct or What Calamities may We not expect, if from an unseasonable parsimony We boldly look on while they are Cut to Pieces. The Boundless Ambition of the Common Enemy and Cruel Rage of their Savage allies now upon our Borders flushed with victory indespensably require a Vigorous and immediate Exertion of all Powers to check their Progress."[1] A fund for defense was recommended, and the Assembly responded promptly to the earnest appeals of their Governor, by acting upon his suggestion without delay. A vote of £6000 current money was passed in aid of Virginia, and assented to by Governor Sharpe. Dinwiddie writes his congratulations to Sharpe, saying: "Washington's defeat has caused more than a victory, it has roused the spirits of our neighboring colonies."[2] But notice that the ways and means[3] provided for raising this fund include ordinary licenses and a tax of one pound sterling on every imported convict.[4] At the time this supply was passed Sharpe had instructions not to assent to any bill

---

[1] Assembly Proceedings, 1754, July 17.
[2] Sharpe Correspondence, I., p. 76.
[3] Assembly Proceedings, 1754, July 25; Bacon's Laws, 1754, ch. 9.
[4] See below, p. 40.

appropriating the ordinary licenses. But necessity and the knowledge that a supply could not be secured any other way induced the Governor and his Council to yield to the Lower House. Sharpe begged the indulgence of his lordship and pleaded urgency as his excuse. Baltimore, on the contrary, far from being gratified at the behavior of his province, was displeased at the public appropriation of the license fees; and although he had nothing to lose, for he had never received this revenue as long as he had been Lord Baltimore, nevertheless Frederick did not become reconciled to the loss of this prospective revenue until September 9, 1755. The Assembly had gained its point and now became more determined than ever. In the meantime, Sharpe was making the best use of his resources. He raised a company of one hundred men and sent them to Wills Creek to engage with other colonial troops in the erection of Fort Cumberland. This fort was erected to serve as an outpost for the frontier defense and as a base of supplies for expeditions against Fort Duquesne. Sharpe, contemplating an attack upon the French stronghold, sought again the assistance of his Assembly, and in December, 1754, the Lower House passed a supply of £7000 to be provided by an emission of "notes of credit." But the provisions for sinking the same contained the old clauses concerning ordinary licenses and imported convicts, which Sharpe, in obedience to his instructions, was bound to reject. Again, in February, 1755, the Lower House voted a supply "for his Majesty's service," this time £10,000, with the foreknowledge, no doubt, that the bill would not become a law. It contained the same provisions that were before objected to by the Proprietary and was rejected. But the Lower House responded by resolving that "they would not grant a Shilling by any other means"; consequently Sharpe's project could not be carried out. These controversies between the representatives of the people and the agents of the Proprietor caused the defeat of effective legislation. Many of the Councillors and the Governor were wavering in their belief that Lord Baltimore's claim to the ordinary licenses was a just one, but the instructions of his Lordship compelled them to act as they did. At the same time the Lower House was determined not to retreat from ground they had gained, and continued to dictate the uses to which the license fund should be put; therefore nothing could be accomplished except by yielding to the House of Delegates. This was a bitter pill for his Lordship, but he had to take it at last.

The question of foreign immigration has always been an important one in America. In the very infancy of Maryland the danger of unrestricted immigration was perceived, and laws were passed to regulate it and keep out undesirable immigrants, among whom were reckoned negroes, Irish papists, and convicts. Considerable revenue was raised from the first two classes. By an early law all imported negroes were bound to service and made slaves for life.[1] In 1695 an imposition of ten shillings per poll, afterwards increased to forty, was placed on all negroes imported, while the same law placed a tax of only two shillings sixpence on white servants.[2] In 1704 a poll of twenty shillings, afterwards doubled, was imposed on the importation of Irish servants, " to prevent too many Irish papists being imported " into the province. These duties were continued throughout the history of the colony, except the tax on Protestant servants, which was repealed in 1732. The Assembly had no complaint to make of these immigrants; but with the importation of convicts it was different, for other questions were involved, and of the three classes, "imported convicts" were the most obnoxious. It appears that the importation of convicts began at an early date. The attention of the Assembly being soon called to this matter, steps were immediately taken to prevent the influx of these undesirable people. An act for that purpose was passed by the Assembly in 1676: " Whereas it had come to their knowledge that severall no-

---

[1] Assem. Proceedings, III., 203.
[2] Called " indented servants."

torious felons and malefactors, taken from the 'Comon Jayles,' had been imported and sold in this province as servants . . . it was provided that a law be enacted to prevent their landing . . . under a forfeit of 2000 pounds of tobacco by the Ship Master in each case."[1] It had been the custom to transport criminals convicted of theft, perjury or forgery, which were then capital offenses, to the colonies, to be there sold into servitude for seven or fourteen years, according to the enormity of their crimes. Their importation to Virginia was first begun by James I., but was soon extended to all the colonies alike. Virginia passed laws to fix a small liability upon their masters for good behavior, while Maryland prohibited their importation outright. The act of 1676 was continued by several reviving acts, and in 1692 a new law was passed, its object being to prevent the landing of convicts. However, their importation to America increased under George I., when the number of offenses for which a criminal was transportable was largely extended. In the meantime the law of 1692 had expired, and even during the continuance of the prohibitive acts no doubt many convicts were smuggled in. In 1723 the Maryland Assembly took the matter up again and passed an "act to prevent the evils arising from the importation of convicts and the better discovery of such when imported." Though passed by both branches of the Legislature, it was vetoed by Lord Baltimore. The reason alleged for shipping the convicts to the colonies was "the great want of servants" there. Hence these criminals, whose services to England were impaired or unnecessary, were sent abroad that they "might be the means of improving his majesties plantations by their labor and industry." Many of the colonies were incensed at this; Pennsylvania put a poll-tax on them as early as 1729, and New York raised a great hue and cry against their importation.[2] "We want people, 'tis true," they said, "but not

---

[1] Assem. Proceedings, II. (1666-1676), p. 540: "An Act against the Importation of Convicted Persons into this Province."
[2] Pitkin, United States, I., 134, 135.

villains, ready at any time, encouraged by impunity, and habituated, upon the slightest occasion, to cut a man's throat for a small part of his property." Similar utterances appeared in the *Maryland Gazette*,[1] but Maryland had no redress while thus handicapped by her Proprietor. It is estimated that from three to four hundred felons found their way into her territory annually.[2] When the French and Indian War brought its demand for revenue, the Assembly hit upon Pennsylvania's plan and placed a poll-tax or duty of £1 on every convict imported. This duty was imposed primarily for revenue purposes, but moral considerations and the example of Pennsylvania were also causes of its imposition. Here came the rub: the importation of felons was authorized by special acts of Parliament; several shipmasters were contracted with to transport them, and England gladly paid a bounty to get rid of this dangerous class of citizens; aside from this, the contractors derived a large profit from the sale of the convicts and enjoyed a profitable monopoly.[3] Naturally they objected to having it curtailed, and consequently when a duty was imposed on convicts by the Act of 1754 a great cry arose from the contractors against it; they threatened to memorialize Parliament. The duty was objected to by the partisans of the Proprietor, who urged that it clashed with the authority of Parliament and would draw a censure from Great Britain. Lord Mansfield, then Attorney-General, was appealed to; he declared "the colony had no power to make such a law, because it was in direct opposition to the authority of Parliament; furthermore, granting that it were proper, colonial legislatures might with equal propriety lay a tariff upon or even prohibit the importation of all English goods." He threatened that unless Lord Baltimore dissented to the Maryland act he would

---

[1] Maryland Gazette, July 30 and August 20, 1767.
[2] Pitkin, United States, I., 133.
[3] The convicts were sold at prices ranging from eight to twenty pounds sterling apiece, though £6 was considered a good premium.

"severely proceed" against it. This opinion was certainly faulty and was based upon the general ground of expediency. If Lord Mansfield had taken the pains to examine the charter he would have found that to Maryland was reserved the exclusive right of levying duties upon commodities imported into the province; and if he had examined the records he would have found old laws actually prohibiting the importation of criminals. Maryland had a moral as well as a legal right to impose such a tariff. Gov. Sharpe, however, advised Baltimore to dissent to the act, giving the Attorney-General's opinion as his reason for such action, if he thought it would involve him in trouble with the Crown. This was not done, but the opinion, though given by the Attorney in his capacity as a private lawyer, and in nowise binding on the Assembly, was used to prevent the placing of duties on imported convicts in other supply bills. The duty of £1 was collected until the £6000 were sunk, and though it was virtually borne by the purchasers of servants, every subsequent attempt by the Lower House to tax convicts was opposed.

3.—The Paper Money Controversy.

About this time another important issue sprang up—the paper money controversy. Paper currency became an important circulating medium of the Province in 1733.[1] Tobacco had always been the general medium of exchange, though other commodities were used, for instance, powder and shot, and payment in kind was common. Tobacco, however, was the most serviceable and obtainable and was never superseded in Maryland during her entire colonial period. The production of tobacco increased greatly and its value depreciated in consequence; English money and other foreign coins were almost entirely driven from the Province. This fact explains the concessions that the Assembly was so willing to make down to 1733 in tobacco duties in return

---

[1] Scharf's Maryland, I., 273-280.

for a commutation of the Proprietary quit-rents. Attempts were made to keep English money in circulation, but without much success. Numerous foreign coins circulated in Maryland and laws were passed from time to time fixing the rates of exchange. But, on the whole, the currency of the province was in a confused state. In 1731, to relieve trade and secure a more stable and convenient medium of exchange, an emission of paper money was proposed, and an act was passed to emit £36,000 in " bills of credit"; not being approved by the Proprietor, it was never enforced. But the Proprietary consent was won over in 1733 when an act was passed "for Emitting and Making Current, Ninety Thousand Pounds . . . in Bills of Credit." This amount was struck, and the act provided that it should circulate for thirty-one years from September 29, 1733, and should be a legal tender in the province for nearly all payments; exceptions being clergy dues, tobacco and tonnage duties and other moneys payable to the Lord Proprietary. All " fees, levies and other duties," however, might be discharged in bills of credit, allowing the difference of £33½ per hundred between sterling and currency.[1] This made the £90,000 equivalent to £60,000 sterling. Various provisions were made to put the act into effect. A loan office was provided and three commissioners or trustees were appointed to superintend the payment and redemption of this currency, to keep account of all money passing through their hands and to receive securities for money loaned. For the redemption of this paper currency a duty of one shilling and threepence was placed on all exported tobacco for thirty-one years. The last clause fixed the periods for the redemption of the bills, two dates being set; the first, September 29, 1748, to March 29, 1749; during this time all bills brought to the loan office were to be cancelled and new bills issued to the value of two-thirds thereof, the other one-third being redeemed. It was expected that all old bills would be replaced by new ones at this first payment, though

---

[1] Bacon's Laws of Maryland, 1733, ch. VI.

there was no obligation to that effect. However, the final redemption of the residue of the bills in circulation was fixed for September 19, 1764, the expiration of the thirty-one years, the statutory limit. This clause is an important one, as we shall see, for it was the cause of much contention between the two houses of Assembly in 1755. At first, on account of the lack of confidence felt by the people in the fund provided for its redemption, paper money rapidly depreciated until £230 currency was only worth £100 sterling. But as soon as the people became convinced of the "goodness of the fund," and when, in 1748, one-third was actually redeemed, the bills rose in value, and by 1753 £150 currency passed for £100 sterling.[1]

It seems that in 1748, the first period provided for redemption, all outstanding paper bills were not presented for reissue. Only £85,984 14s. were brought in, an amount lacking £4015 6s. of the original issue. "Some of the Politicians," says Sharpe, "who out of their singular regard for the Pocketts of their Constituents and perhaps their own Interest"[2] discovered that fact and proposed to make use of it to embarrass the government. A large majority of the House of Delegates were persuaded that the £4000 in question were destroyed by fire or other accidents, and that a new issue to the same amount would not affect the value of the currency, for it would not increase the sum provided for by the Paper Currency Act. While the exigencies of the time might have justified a reasoning after this fashion, yet it was treading dangerous ground to legislate upon a supposition. There was little evidence that this amount of paper had been destroyed; on the contrary, there was reason to believe that a great deal of it was still in circulation, for small quantities were held by people living at considerable distances from the seat of government, who did not think it worth their while to make a special trip to the Loan Office

---
[1] Sharpe Correspondence, I., 138, etc.
[2] Sharpe Correspondence, I., 162.

to have a small amount exchanged.¹ When the bill for £7000 was passed by the Lower House it was provided that £4015 6s. of it should be a new issue of the paper money office.² This was rejected by the Council for the reasons mentioned, and because it was thought dangerous to establish a precedent that might have led to other measures having for their effect the debasement of the currency. Maryland did not stand alone in this controversy, for New York and New Jersey had also refused to vote supplies except they be allowed a new emission of paper currency, and royal instructions prevented their governors from consenting to this. Pennsylvania likewise was very anxious to "strike more paper." In Maryland the paper money controversy created a serious obstruction and blocked tighter than ever the wheels of administration.

4.—Refusal of the Proprietary to share the Burdens of Taxation.

Since the voting and expenditure of the supply of £6000, three fruitless sessions of the Assembly had been wasted in unsuccessful efforts to put the province in a state of defense. Their work was dissipated in disputes over ordinary licenses, imported convicts and the paper currency. Sharpe's urgent appeals were in vain, and the Lower House remained firm in the conviction of the justice of its course. Neither side was willing to make any concessions to the other, and no agreement was reached between the administration and the delegates. All the while reports were sent from Fort Cumberland to the Governor concerning the frequent depredations and murders which were committed by the Indians among the "back inhabitants,"³ as the people in the western part of the province were called. These distressing facts were laid

---

[1] A rise in the value of the currency at this time would tend to give further credence to this view.
[2] The remainder was provided for by special taxes.
[3] Sharpe Correspondence, I., 365.

before the Assembly by the Governor, and the Lower House recommended a company of rangers to picket the frontier and £1500 for their support; but the bill failed, presumably because it contained a clause placing an additional tax of five shillings on imported convicts. As there was no news from Braddock and further delay was dangerous, Sharpe secured a small company of volunteers and hastened to Fort Cumberland. While on his way thither a report of Braddock's defeat reached him,[1] occasioning great surprise and producing the wildest commotion among the settlers. A private subscription had been raised by the members of the Council and other gentlemen of the province; this was all Sharpe could count upon, and out of it he garrisoned several forts or places of refuge for the people of Frederick County, and supported at Fort Cumberland Dagworthy's company, the only body of Maryland troops that had accompanied the Braddock expedition. Every effort was made by Sharpe to quiet the panic-stricken inhabitants and strengthen the frontier defense. To say that he was partially successful is a tribute to his executive ability, for Sharpe was left to cope with the situation almost alone. As it was, a large number of the western inhabitants left their homes and fled to Baltimore and other places. Fort Cumberland was merely the pretense of a fortification and was too far west to be of service in protecting the province. If the French on the Ohio had not changed their tactics at this juncture the consequences might have been serious. The Indians made several though unsuccessful attempts to capture Fort Cumberland. In the meantime Lord Baltimore became aroused for the safety of his western lands and bowed to the resolutions of the Assembly; he yielded his claims[2] to the ordinary licenses and hawkers' and pedlers' licenses as well, as soon as the news of Braddock's defeat reached him,[3] and issued instructions to his Lieutenant-Governor to pass any

---

[1] July 15, 1755. See also above, p. 24.
[2] £640 per annum. Sharpe Cor., I., 368.
[3] Sept. 9, 1755.

act of the Assembly for a money loan which appropriated these licenses for the "common cause." The Lord Proprietary flattered himself that his concessions would settle all misunderstanding between the administration and the legislature; but he was mistaken. It was easily seen that this concession had been forced from his Lordship reluctantly. Far from being a great favor, it was an acknowledgment of the power and authority of the Lower House of the Provincial Assembly.

By patience and determination the House of Delegates had won its issue with the Proprietary, though five or six almost fruitless sessions had been spent in the effort. The Proprietor had lost through undue interference with the right, which the province had now acquired, to levy its own taxes and control public revenues. The long disputes over imported convicts, paper money, and especially ordinary licenses had aroused discontent with the Proprietary administration, indifference for the English government that supported its policy, and led the representatives of the people to prejudice their own safety to maintain their liberty.

After this broadside had taken effect the Lower House aimed another. The vantage-ground they had gained emboldened them to attack the personal or private rights of the Lord Proprietary. This leads us to the fourth cause of Maryland's inactivity in the French and Indian War: that is, the refusal of the Proprietary to share the burdens of the war and waive the right to have his estates exempted from taxation.

During the autumn of 1755 nothing was done to check the depredations and outrages of the Indians on the frontier, for the Assembly was not called together again until February, 1756. Gov. Shirley, of Massachusetts, had succeeded to the chief command of the American forces after the death of Braddock. A council of war was held in New York in December, 1755, where the plans for 1756 were decided.[1]

---
[1] Sharpe Cor., I., 315-320.

While the scene of action was transferred to the Canada border, it was left to the tact of Governor Sharpe, who was appointed commander for the Southern colonies, to organize an expedition against Fort Duquesne. There existed the old desire to recover this American fort and overawe their Indian enemies, at whose hands they suffered more than from the French, for the Indians had improved the opportunity for plunder offered by French successes. To cope with such a state of things the activity and coöperation of the colonies were imperative. In Maryland, as in Pennsylvania, the force of public opinion was also brought to bear upon the provincial government to induce speedy action. With the hope that the pressure of circumstances might have the desired effect on the Assembly, Sharpe called it together again, February 23, 1756. The Assembly appeared willing to grant supplies, provided it could have its own way in directing the measures for raising them. After a delay of nearly two months, a supply of £40,000 was voted by the Lower House. To raise this large grant taxes were placed upon a variety of commodities, imports and exports; even bachelors and billiard tables were not omitted; while taxes imposed by previous acts, notably that of 1754, were continued by this act of 1756.[1] With unswerving constancy the Lower House included all the objectionable features of former supply bills and a few more besides, such as the duty on imported convicts, ordinary licenses, new emissions of paper money and a land tax. The last was distinctly a new feature, for it was the first tax on land ever imposed and collected in Maryland; but the great demand for revenue necessitated recourse to such a tax. The bill met with a stormy reception. "Too much dictation by the Lower House," objected the Council. It is true the delegates had prescribed rather minutely the purposes for which each portion of the money should be appropriated, and left but little to the discretion of the Governor except to see that they were properly carried

---

[1] Bacon's Laws of Maryland, 1756, ch. V.

out. The Lower House had acquired powers over money bills equal to those of the House of Commons, and this was a practical assertion of them. The duty on convicts, the emission of paper money and the land tax got their share of opprobrium. These were "some" of the reasons for the rejection of the bill by the Upper House. But the delegates were firm in resisting nearly every attempted compromise of their schemes and plans, and often allowed the debate to fall away into parliamentary quibbling, in which the real points at issue were lost sight of. A second and a third time the same bill for a supply of £40,000, with a few slight modifications, was passed by the Lower House and as often rejected by the Upper. The delegates assumed too great a power over the settling of the land tax, it was objected; after what manner we shall see.

One of the most important measures introduced into this bill was the provision that a small tax, one shilling per hundred acres, should be imposed on all freehold estates, and the Proprietary lands as well.[1] The Lord Proprietary was lord and owner of the soil, and in virtue of these rights his lands were beyond the control of the Assembly. Lord Baltimore held a large quantity of vacant land in the western part of the province. Frederick, who was only anxious to swell his

---

[1] The lands of the Lord Proprietary were of three classes, manor, reserved, and vacant lands. The manor lands were large tracts, held by the Lord Proprietor, that had been properly surveyed and a description of whose bounds and general features had been entered upon the public records. They were leased in parcels to tenants. The reserved lands were tracts of territory which were ordered to be held in reserve for the Proprietor, on account of their fertility, mineral wealth, contiguity to his manors or towns. These reserved lands had not been surveyed nor laid out, nor designated by any particular name, as the manors were; but like the manor lands they were rented in portions by his Lordship's agents, who were forbidden to sell or gran them to any one. All other lands owned by the Proprietor, notably those in the western part of the province and on the frontier, and which were open at the Land Office to purchase by any one at the "common rates," were called vacant lands. These afforded no immediate revenue. Sharpe Cor., I., 426.

income, urged Sharpe repeatedly to advance the price of his western lands and the rents of his manors; but the insecurity of the western border diminished the number of applications for this land, and in consequence it was difficult to raise the price of that for which there was little sale. The Proprietary gave no assistance to his province in these trying times, and in this instance one can hardly help excusing the Assembly for regarding Frederick as an obstacle that had to be conquered. In the tax upon land his manor and reserved lands were included, and in this way Baltimore was made to contribute a small portion at least towards the defense of his own province. Had Frederick come promptly forward to the relief of the people with a modest contribution he might have created a loyal feeling among them and have saved himself many vexatious encroachments upon his rights. The first attempt to tax the Proprietary in Pennsylvania was responded to by the Penns with a contribution of £5000. Furthermore, the safety of the province settled, the value of his western land would be restored; as Sharpe tried to convince him, the annual loss to his Lordship was at this time much greater than the tax proposed upon his estates. Therefore it could only be short-sighted policy to hamper the Governor with instructions that led Sharpe to entertain "no sanguine hopes of the bill." His Lordship was afraid of adding another precedent to those which had already marked the downfall of his feudal prerogatives. Sharpe again expressed his former conviction that it must be left to Parliament to step in and "save the Assembly the trouble of providing for its own safety." However, the more Baltimore resisted, the weaker his position grew: a conference of the two branches resulted in a satisfactory agreement upon the bill.

In the meantime a change of sentiment had taken place among the councillors of the administration; it was considered futile to oppose the Lower House further at this time and thereby jeopard the safety of the province; consequently, Sharpe, aided by the persuasion of the Proprietary Council, came to the conclusion that it was best to assent to the bill if passed again, even though it contained the objectionable tax upon Lord Baltimore's land. His excuses were "the preservation of his province," the loss in Proprietary revenue, and the parsimony of Frederick himself. In regard to the latter, Sharpe said: "If an Act of Generosity in his Ldp had afforded me the least Room I would not have despaired of making them [*i. e.* the Assembly] ashamed of their Behaviour and of rendering them odious to their own Constituents." In the conference between the two branches of the legislature many trifling objections were adjusted. The duty on imported convicts was excepted, an additional land tax was provided for to supply any deficiency that might occur in the sinking fund, and above all it was mutually agreed that Lord Baltimore's manors and rent-paying reserved lands should bear a tax equal to that imposed upon lands patented or granted by the Lords Proprietary to the inhabitants of the province, while his other lands should be exempted. The bill for a supply of £40,000 was passed May 14, 1756, after thirteen weeks of delay and dispute. Sharpe took the situation philosophically, though he expressed his disapproval of the Assembly's conduct. Conscious that "the Lower House would not let the Lives of a few inhabitants come in Competition with their Schemes and Views," anxious alike for the safety of the province and the increase of his lord's revenues, Sharpe took the advice of the Proprietary Council and assented to the land tax. He had acted contrary to Baltimore's wishes. It was not without "some Apprehentions," said he, "that this Step ... would be censured as a culpable Concession and subversive of His Ldp's Rights and prerogatives"; but the security of the province was his first duty, and Sharpe yielded.

Frederick's indecision had decided Sharpe in the course he took, and upon it he felt willing to stake his reputation with the Lord Proprietary.[1] Although Sharpe was advised to

---

[1] Sharpe Cor., I., 399.

follow in the path of Governor Morris of Pennsylvania, in "guarding against any Invasion of Proprietary rights and prerogatives," he received no definite and peremptory instructions upon the issues between Lord Baltimore and the people. Governor Sharpe had solicited instructions to remove the "uncertainty," and stood ready to execute them though he should be called by the people "an Odious Instrument" for so doing. Lord Baltimore's revenue the past year had fallen £1600 below what it had been the year previous, and this was attributed to the abandonment of the western lands and their depreciation in value; while, on the contrary, the Proprietary land tax, for the five years to which it was limited, only amounted to £400. "Was His Ldp's Case my own," writes the Governor at the time, "I am sure I would never have hesitated a moment to contribute my Share with the people to defend the province and annoy the Enemy."[1] It is clear that a liberal stroke on the part of Lord Baltimore, a modest but sympathetic contribution, would likely have saved him considerable embarrassment. By the act of 1756 the Assembly scored another point against Proprietary rule.

5.—PENNSYLVANIA'S INFLUENCE UPON MARYLAND.

Let us turn for a moment to Pennsylvania to see the influence exerted by her upon Maryland. The conduct of both provinces with regard to the land tax was very similar, for each had the same interests at stake and the same kind of a government. Sharpe watched the course of Pennsylvania's Assembly closely and reported every favorable move to his own legislative body, hoping in the event of his neighbors passing an "acceptable bill" that Maryland's Assembly would be influenced to become "Imitators of the Quakers' conduct."

General Braddock's defeat was as much of a surprise to the Pennsylvanians as it was to Marylanders. They, too, had practically left the British to fight their own battles, but

---

[1] Sharpe Cor., I., 427.

the Assembly was now sufficiently aroused to pass a vote of £50,000. To raise this sum the General Assembly proposed a tax of "twelve pence per pound and twenty shillings per Head, Yearly for two Years, on all the Estates real and personal, and Taxables" within the province. All the lands of the Proprietaries as well as those of the people were included. This proposition was made July 30, 1755, and it fell with the effect of a bombshell upon the Proprietors. It looked to them like an effort to destroy their authority. The measure aimed in particular at the vacant lands held by the Proprietary, and with some reason, too. Governor Morris, in obedience to his instructions, opposed the proposition with all his skill in argument. The position of the people was based upon equity and common benefit. It is but fair, said the Assembly, since we are called upon to defend the Proprietary estates on the frontier, that our Proprietors should bear their share of the burdens. The opposition of the administration to this measure was based on prerogative, precedent and law. Says Governor Morris: 1. "All Governors, from the nature of their office, are exempt from the payment of taxes." 2. "This exemption is supported by a positive law of the province; for a law of the province, investing the assessors with power to assess and lay taxes in the several counties, contains an express proviso that the Proprietary estates should not be taxed." 3. "It is contrary to the constant practice and usage of this and all other Proprietary Governments to lay any tax upon the lands or estates of the Proprietaries exercising the government by themselves or their lieutenants."[1] The Assembly asserted a right to tax the Proprietors as landlords and not as governors, and requested Gov. Morris not to "make himself the hateful Instrument of reducing a free people to the abject state of Vassalage." "What Laws of Imposition," said he, ". . . have I attempted to force down your Throats?"

---

[1] Pennsylvania Colonial Records, VI., 525, 526.
[2] Pennsylvania Colonial Records, VI., 584.

The Assembly responds: "A Law to Tax the people of Pennsylvania To defend the Proprietary Estate, and to exempt the Proprietary Estate from bearing any part of the Tax, is, may it please the Governor, a Law abhorrent to common Justice, common Reason and common Sense." While the Administration had law and precedent on its side, the proposition of the Assembly seems to have been fair and just. Thus did the burgesses express their feelings toward Proprietary rule, for they were determined to endanger the safety of the colony, if necessary, to attain their ends. Governor Morris came forward with a compromise and proposed to grant bounty lands to those who would volunteer for the expedition against the French. Lands west of the Alleghanies were to be given, without purchase money and free from the payment of quit-rents for fifteen years, and then not to exceed the common quit-rent[1] of the province. But this did not satisfy the Assembly, and judging from the tone of their messages, they deemed it almost an impertinence in the Governor to have suggested an alternative to their measure. Consequently the bill for £50,000 fell through. Shortly after, another bill, appropriating £60,000 for the same purpose and with substantially the same provisions, was proposed. Governor Morris could not give his assent to this bill. He was firm with the Assembly and faithful to his superiors; but he was honest enough to confess that the Proprietors' real reason for not yielding to the tax upon their lands was "to preserve the rights of their Station; if they gave up these they would soon be stript of everything they had a right to enjoy, both power and property."[3] The Governor then expressed a desire that the Penns be taxed by Parliament, if they were to be taxed at all, "for if the power is ever given into the hands of the people here," he wrote, "they will use it without mercy."[4]

---

[1] 4s. 2d. sterling.
[2] Nov. 6, 1755.
[3] Pa. Col. Records, VI., 544.
[4] Pa. Col. Records, VI., 738-9.

But the perseverance of the Assembly bore good fruit. In the meanwhile the Proprietors had been informed of the defeat of Braddock, the insecurity of the province and the doings of the Assembly. Governor Morris's conduct was commended and the Proprietors, in order to settle the dispute, offered a contribution of £5000 with a proviso that their estates should be exempted from taxation. While this was proffered as a free gift and not as a commutation for their share of the Assembly's appropriation, Morris was instructed that if the burgesses provided simply the difference, £55,000, he should not insist upon the balance.[1] This is significant; the Assembly interpreted it as a concession on the part of the Proprietaries, and this it certainly was. The gift was accepted and the bill for £60,000 passed November 26, 1755, but the Assembly provided only for the striking of £55,000 in bills of credit, the remainder being supplied by the gift of £5000 which was accepted in lieu of a tax upon the Proprietary estates.[2] Although the administration thought it had staved off the idea of taxing the lands of the Proprietary, the people had won a real victory. In the interim the people of Maryland were watching Pennsylvania closely, and so was Sharpe; he was awaiting the turn of the tide. If their Assembly passed a suitable bill he intended calling together his own; on the other hand, unfavorable action by his neighbor would make it useless, so the Governor of Maryland thought; for he was confident that if Pennsylvania set an ill example Maryland would be sure to follow it.[3] But the passage of £60,000 in the autumn of 1755 gave him fresh hope. Consequently, he called his Assembly together early in 1756 and expected a ready response. In this he was partially disappointed, as we know, for the Mary-

---

[1] Pa. Col. Records, VI., 731.
[2] The bill was not satisfactory, but passed the Council because of the restlessness of the people for some definite action. Pa. Col. Records, VI., 734; also VI., 737-738.
[3] Sharpe Cor., I., 269.

land Assembly adopted Pennsylvania's tactics. The landtax was again the bugbear, and the Governor and his council were forced to reject the first proposal to grant £40,000. At this period Maryland and Pennsylvania had the same controversies, but the tax proposed in Maryland was quite different from the so-called "pound-tax"[1] of Pennsylvania. For instance, the latter included all the Proprietaries' personal and real estate in the province, which was taxed and assessed according to its value, *i. e.* at the rate of 12d. per £, by such assessors as the people should elect. Maryland, on the contrary, proposed a specific tax of 1s. per hundred acres, which embraced the Proprietary manor and reserved lands,[2] but excluded the vacant lands. The Lower House even receded from this, as we have seen, and agreed to tax only those parts of his lordship's reserved lands which were actually leased out and paid a rent; the remainder being classed with the vacant lands. Thus Maryland's proposition was different from that of Pennsylvania and far more reasonable. Nevertheless it was treated with more indifference by Lord Baltimore than was shown by the Penns.[3] This may partly account for the easy victory which the Assembly gained over the administration in March, 1756, for a solution of the difficulty was forced upon Governor Sharpe by Frederick's in lecision. In truth, Maryland scored a victory before her neighbor, and her example reacted by way of encouragement upon Pennsylvania. In the meantime William Denny had succeeded Morris as Governor of Pennsylvania.[4] The Assembly tried its persuasive powers upon him with a bill to grant £100,000 for the King's service, including in its provisions a tax upon the estates of the Proprietaries. This bill was rejected; but Governor Denny

---

[1] *i. e.* 12 pence per £, and 20 shillings per head.

[2] See above, p. 50, note.

[3] For as soon as the Penns received Gov. Morris's letter of July 30, 1755, they ordered a contribution of £5000. Pa. Col. Records, VI., 730.

[4] August, 1756.

was more plastic in the hands of the Assembly than Morris and in due time they were able to win him to their own schemes.

Benjamin Franklin was at this time a leader in the Assembly. So powerful was his influence and so effectually did he champion the views of the Assembly that he was even accused by the administration of trying to take the government out of the hands of the Proprietaries. It was now determined to send a representative to England to present their grievances, and Franklin was selected [2] as the fittest advocate to exonerate the Assembly before Parliament and expose the "Iniquity of the Proprietary Instructions." He arrived in London July 27, 1757, and wisely resolved to see the Proprietaries first. Before them he laid the complaints of the Pennsylvanians, the most important of which, we remember, was the question concerning the taxing of the Proprietors' estates. Franklin was referred to their solicitor, Ferdinand John Paris, "a proud, angry man," as Pennsylvania's representative termed him. Franklin refused to deal with any one but the Penns themselves. His petition was referred to the Attorney-General for the latter's opinion. What the Attorney's opinion was, if he gave any, Franklin never learned, but about a year later the Proprietaries "sent a long message to the Assembly," says Franklin, "drawn up and signed by Paris, reciting my paper, . . . giving a flimsy justification of their conduct, adding that they should be willing to accommodate matters if the Assembly would send out some person of candour to treat with them for that purpose, intimating thereby that I was not such." [3]

In the meantime Governor Denny had yielded to the pressure upon him; he had been persuaded by the Assembly to pass an act,[4] wherein the estates of the Proprietaries were

---

[1] Pa. Col. Records, VI., 739.
[2] Feb., 1757.
[3] Franklin's Works, I., p. 298 (J. Bigelow edition).
[4] For £100,000, passed in April, 1759. The estates of the Proprietors were assessed and taxed by assessors of the people's choosing. By this

taxed in common with those of the people. This was the grand rallying point of all their disputes, and now that the Assembly had carried the provincial administration with them, instead of responding to the message of the Proprietaries, they sent over the act itself for confirmation. The Proprietaries determined to prevent it from receiving the royal assent and employed able counsel to argue their case. Franklin now appeared before the Board of Trade[1] to defend the Pennsylvania Assembly, but they reported unfavorably upon the act. However, the act was afterwards reviewed before the King in Council, and through the aid of Lord Mansfield the report of the Lords of Trade was reversed.[2] Indeed, the Assembly had anticipated the order of Council by the levy of one year's tax under the act in question. Pennsylvania's victory over her Proprietaries was decisive.

Act the Proprietaries were subjected to the same taxes as were laid upon other lands by the several Acts that were passed after 1754. The Act was to continue for twelve years, and it was estimated that within that time the Lords Proprietary would be made to pay about £72,000.

[1] May, 1760.
[2] Franklin's Works, I., p. 300 (Bigelow's ed.). Bancroft's United States, II., 529-530.

CONCLUSION.

DAWN OF INDEPENDENCE.

From Governor Sharpe's correspondence we learn the real motives of the Assembly's actions. His letters to his own brothers, in particular, contain calm and disinterested surveys of Maryland politics at that time. It is clear that Maryland failed in the duty she owed her sister provinces and the mother-country, and were there no circumstances to explain this fact her behavior would be inexcusable.

Indifference and "unseasonable parsimony" are the first causes that occur to us. It was with the greatest difficulty, we remember, that the province was brought to a sense of her danger when the French were occupying the Ohio Valley, and not until Washington's surrender were they induced to vote a supply. They "looked on the incursions of their ambitious and insulting enemies,"[1] says Sharpe, "with the greatest indifference." The Assembly was excessively frugal and they objected to being burdened with taxes. Only small sums were voted, and when to save appearances apparently liberal bills passed the Lower House they were clogged with provisions that prevented them from becoming laws. This is also seen in the unwillingness of Maryland to take any aggressive steps or to carry war outside of her own territory. All that was done was confined to the defense of the frontier and the fortification of the province against invasion. The Assembly would pass no effective militia law nor provide equipment for the provincial troops, and it not only refused to allow its troops to go beyond its own borders except in the pay of Great Britain, but also neglected to support the garrisons within the province. When in 1758 the French with-

---

[1] Sharpe Cor., I., 109.

drew from the Ohio Valley and the Southern colonies were out of danger, Sharpe wrote to Baltimore: "As the Inhabitants of the Province ... are not ambitious of acquiring a Reputation for Zeal and exemplary Loyalty, they seem to be very indifferent about the Event of the Campaign."[1] We may even go a step further and say that the Assembly or many of the leading men acted disloyally, for the Governor, in his efforts to raise money from the people by private subscriptions, was opposed by the Burgesses, who endeavored to persuade the people that if money were raised by such methods they must expect to do without Assemblies and abide by ordinances rather than "Laws made ... with their own consent." "With the empty sounds of Liberty and Priveledge," says Sharpe, "... these Tribunes impose on the weak minds of the people ... while ... they effectually contribute to their Destruction." The refusal of the Assembly to support Dagworthy and his company at Fort Cumberland and the reduction of the already small provincial force to 300 in 1757 seem inexcusable. One member of the Assembly, it is said, went among the soldiers and told them that since no money had been raised to pay them they were not obliged to continue in the service, and that if they did the Assembly would never agree to pay them. Moreover, their treatment of royal requisitions and their conduct toward the Roman Catholics showed clearly their temper towards all dictation. The system known as "Crown Requisitions" was imposed by the English government upon the colonies at an early date. It was the first scheme introduced by the Crown to raise money in the provinces for the conduct of border warfare. A royal requisition to each Governor prescribed the quota of men and supplies expected. The system was obnoxious to the colonies, and especially to Maryland, for the charter of the latter contained ample provisions against royal interference with the autonomy of the province. Requisitions were sent to Maryland as early as

---

[1] Sharpe Cor., II., 397.

1694, but, despite their imperative character, they were commonly received with indifference and met a dogged resistance. Maryland held that "no taxes or imposition of any kind could be laid without the assent of the General Assembly," and the Assembly endeavored to prevent any infraction of this chartered privilege.[1] Even during the suspension of Proprietary government (1689–1715) the Royal government only obtained its levies with the consent of the Assembly. Maryland pursued the same policy during the French and Indian War, as we have seen. The plan for a general union of his Majesty's northern colonies for defense and the "common fund" had both failed. Braddock's requisitions were treated with contempt, and he not only received but little assistance from Maryland and Pennsylvania, but was hampered by them besides. Maryland failed to support properly the small company furnished for his expedition,[2] and repeated mutterings of discontent were heard from the people and in the Assembly against Braddock's troops for their unscrupulous conduct in appropriating at will large numbers of servants, carriages and horses. Some of the governors applied to England for an act of Parliament to compel the colonies to contribute their quotas, and Calvert, Baltimore's secretary, wrote Sharpe the warning: "it wo^d be Best the Americans did not Subject themselves to Tax from hence"[3]—a threat rash and unheeded, as subsequent history proves. Governor Sharpe again brought forward his pet idea of a general poll-tax enforced by Parliament, for he was convinced that nothing but a compulsory act by Parliament could "effectually preserve the Colonies from ruin."[4] While the disputes with the Proprietary explain largely the apathy in Maryland toward the mother-country, it does not account for it fully. The province was

---

[1] As early as 1698 Maryland maintained that no law of England should be binding upon them without their consent.

[2] Sharpe advanced £100 from his own pocket for the purpose. Sharpe Cor., I., 245.

[3] Sharpe Cor., I., 135.

[4] Sharpe Cor., II., 85-86.

always jealous of her rights, and the charter was the standard by which she measured her independence of England. Maryland enjoyed most of the privileges of a sovereign state and acted accordingly. It is evident from the legislation of the House of Commons that Parliament was much incensed at the behavior of Maryland. In 1756 (February 3) a grant of £95,000 was made to the "Plantations in North America;" but in the distribution, Virginia, Maryland, Pennsylvania and the two Carolinas were excluded the benefit. Calvert gave the reason to Sharpe in these words: "The Construction had and held of them Province is, they have fail'd of that just regard and not complying to his Majesty's Secy of State, therefore the Legislature here think them at present not of notice to His Majesty."[1] Furthermore, Lord Loudon, when he became commander-in-chief of the American forces (1756–1758), was not able to command the respect and obedience of Maryland's Assembly. They did not listen to his requisitions and scorned all dictation. Contrary to his orders, they resolved to withdraw the garrison from Fort Cumberland, on the frontier of the province, and reduce their force to 300 men; at the same time they refused to allow any Maryland troops to leave the province under his command except they be in his pay. By such legislation the frontier was left ill-protected, and the province would have been in great danger had the French at Fort Duquesne manifested any activity.

With the accession of the Pitt ministry in England in 1758, and the appointment of Amherst to the command of the British forces in America, the tide turned. General Forbes was placed in charge of an expedition against Fort Duquesne, with instructions to secure the active coöperation of the Southern colonies. But the attitude of the Assembly reflects great discredit upon the province. They had refused to maintain the garrison at Fort Cumberland, and the troops, having been without pay for eight months,

---

[1] Quoted as it stands in the Records. Sharpe Cor., I., 370.

or not having "fingered any money," as Sharpe put it, were on the point of disbanding. In order to keep this force together until the close of the campaign General Forbes was obliged to take the 300 men stationed at Fort Cumberland and Fort Frederick into his own pay and advance £1500 for their support upon the credit of the province. In this way they were kept from starving and remained a part of Forbes's army until Fort Duquesne was reclaimed.[1]

After much persuasion the Assembly promised to reimburse Forbes for his advances, but this resolution does not seem to have been fulfilled. Upon the occupation of Fort Duquesne warfare in the south was practically over, and General Amherst, with his aides, Generals Johnson and Wolfe, conducted the war to a successful close in the north; Canada was captured by the British, but without any assistance from Maryland. The entreaties of Pitt and Amherst were of no avail, and Sharpe had to resign himself to the consciousness that the Assembly must be left to its own course.

The treatment of Roman Catholics is an unsavory subject in Maryland history. During the French and Indian War the persecution of this portion of the population continued. Every possible pretext for bringing in bills to restrict their liberties and "prevent the growth of Popery" seems to have been seized upon. Fortunately, however, many of these bills never got beyond the journals of the Lower House. If perchance a person of this faith had secured an appointment to a responsible position a protest would be made "against favors shown to Catholics." Charges were made that they were in collusion with the French, but most of these charges, happily, proved to be malicious lies concocted for the purpose of creating a prejudice against the Roman Catholics. So strong was the sentiment against them that members of the Assembly failed of

---

[1] Nov. 25, 1758.

reëlection on account of their opposition to bills affecting the Catholics. In response to the petitions of the Lower House Sharpe pronounced their behavior "unexceptionable" and said it would be hard to take any measures that might be called persecution.[1]

In 1756, when the vote of £40,000 was passed, a double tax was placed upon the lands of all Roman Catholics; to this there was little objection on the part of the administration, for the reason that Catholics were excused from attending "Musters as Militia."[2] Their petitions to Sharpe to veto the bill and their threats to appeal to the King in Council had no effect. Governor Sharpe, though he confessed that he did not think it so great an injustice, would have prevented the double taxation if he had been able. In the same year in which the double taxation was imposed it was even proposed in the Assembly to disarm all Roman Catholics in the province, and the opposition to this obnoxious measure only prevailed by a slender majority of one.[3] Sharpe's conduct is to be highly commended, for though a Protestant he never allowed himself to be carried away by the intolerant spirit that prevailed. The Governor defended himself against all charges of favoritism in a frank and commendable manner, conscientiously opposed all attempts of the Assembly to persecute the Catholics, and refused to sanction any acts affecting them which were unreasonably severe. Yet, withal, we find no disloyalty among the Catholics. Rather is their treatment a reflection of the character of the Assembly itself and an indication of the general apathy that prevailed in the province in regard to the issue of the struggle for Canada. Instead of spending all its energy to restore the security and dignity of Maryland, the Assembly wasted much of its valuable time in false charges

---

[1] Sharpe Cor., I., 408. Sharpe, though a Protestant himself, said that they were really better than the Protestants.

[2] Sharpe Cor., I., 419-20.

[3] The vote stood 19 to 18. Assem. Proc., Sept., 1756.

and in the passing of laws against the "Papists," attempting to make them, as it were, a subterfuge to shield its own inactivity. We are not surprised, therefore, that Sharpe, as did others, harped incessantly upon the idea of an act of Parliament to compel the colonies, in particular Maryland and Pennsylvania, to help themselves. General Forbes's admonition, "Great Britain will not be blind to their Behaviour . . . on this occasion," was verified in 1765. When, in 1766, Maryland was called to account by the House of Commons, the task of defending her conduct fell upon Franklin, who explained it away as best he could.[1]

Opposition to Proprietary rule existed from the very beginning of the province. The people at the start took the lawmaking power out of the hands of the Proprietor, to whom it was given by the charter; the wisdom of the first Proprietor made him yield to a compromise that was unavoidable. This attitude of the Assembly developed by 1739 "a Political Faction," which opposed the Administration in everything. The Assembly of that year may be truly called an Assembly of grievances.

From henceforward, "no Supplies without redress of grievances" became the rallying principle, and the French and Indian War gave them a glorious opportunity to enforce this principle and extend their encroachments upon his lordship's prerogatives. The Assembly, however, carried their disputes to an extreme not warranted by the grievances themselves, as we have seen in the quarrels over the port duty and the tobacco tax. Many of the burgesses seem to have lost their heads and to have exhausted their powers of logic in their attempts to right fancied wrongs. Again, in the paper money controversy they took a weak stand, and if the Assembly had been given a free rein it would have greatly depreciated the currency of the province. Subservi-

---

[1] Franklin took the view that Maryland's backwardness was the fault of her government and not of her people. Franklin's Works, III., pp. 425-6 (Bigelow's ed.).

ence to the example set by Pennsylvania, permitting the people of the frontier to suffer from constant depredations, allowing the troops to starve without more effective measures of assistance, were evidences of an attitude on the part of the Assembly far from commendable, and Maryland was justly called to account for perverting such an opportunity to the attainment of selfish and ambitious ends.

Something can be said, however, in favor of the independent attitude of Maryland's Assembly. Frederick Calvert's imbecile conduct proved him a man unfit to rule a great province. The Assembly had acquired large privileges which by the charter belonged originally to the Proprietor. Possibly these were gained more by force than by right, but it meant to retain them forever. Out of feudal elements had developed a government by the people too dear to English ideas of independence to be relinquished.

Consequently when Frederick began to interfere with these acquired rights of the province he was unconscious, or if conscious, indifferent to the mistake he was making. He objected to the appropriation of ordinary licenses for the expenses of the war, although his predecessor Charles had readily assented to such appropriations for public purposes on less imperative occasions. He instructed his Lieutenant-Governor to object to the duty on convicts for fear of a censure from the Crown, although previous to this the right to prohibit their importation altogether had been recognized and assented to. The attempt to interfere with the Assembly's taxing powers, which was dictated by a selfish regard for his own interests, made Lord Baltimore very unpopular. Furthermore, his unwillingness to give the grievances of his people a fair hearing, his efforts to smother petitions to the Crown, aggravated the feelings of the provincials and made them all the more determined to resist Proprietary rule. His liberality was again put to the test in 1756 when the Assembly proposed to tax his estates; the result we have already seen. Maryland was less radical than Pennsylvania, and had Frederick even manifested the liberality of the Penns he might have saved his estates. He was a heavy loser by the war, as Sharpe constantly pointed out to him, and economy as well as justice seemed to dictate a generous policy. But here the Proprietary was at fault again, and the Assembly persisted in its schemes.

The design of the Assembly was to limit the authority of the Proprietary in the province and transfer it to the representatives of the people. And Governor Sharpe says of the legislation of the Lower House that it "manifestly tended to deprive the Government of all Power and to throw it entirely into the hands of the People as it is in Pensilvania."[1] This spirit of aggression was not new; it had only been intensified by the indifferent conduct of their Proprietor. Why did Frederick not visit his province nor concern himself about its difficulties, nor inquire as to whether or not the province was able or ought to bear alone the burden of protecting his property? It was because he cared so little for it. Is it any wonder, therefore, that "the Lower House," as Sharpe says, "seemed to be determined to grant no Supplies unless they could at the same time carry certain points which tended to subvert in a great measure the Constitution."[2] No doubt Governor Sharpe's pet term for the Lower House —"a Levelling House of Burgesses"—is an apt one, for they were scheming to belittle and perhaps overthrow their Proprietary government. Frederick's policy was calculated to help rather than hinder this design; it created discord which might have been avoided, and invited the interference of the English Crown in the affairs of the province.

It seems to have been the intention of some of the leading men of the Assembly to play the colony into the hands of the Crown. The object for doing such a thing may be surmised; under Royal government the Assembly anticipated a monopoly of the provincial administration. The events of the next few years show their mistake.

---

[1] Sharpe Cor., II., 177.
[2] Sharpe Cor., I., 391.

Of the indications that point to such a design several are important. Doubtless the remembrance of the Royal government in 1715 was still fresh in mind, and the Assembly thought the Crown a safe retreat from the rule of the Proprietary. We have already seen what an effort the Lower House made in 1739 to petition the king to redress their grievances. Again, in 1756, the Assembly attempted to have their grievances brought before the King in Council, and desired an agent in London to represent them. Lord Baltimore did his utmost to repress anything of this sort, for fear that it "would plunge him into a Sea of Trouble."[1] This opposition increased their hostility towards Proprietary government.

It was Sharpe's belief that it was the object of the leading men of the Assembly "to throw things into confusion" and thus exempt themselves and their constituents from all taxes. Beyond a doubt there was a strong desire on the part of many to bring about some interference on the part of the Crown which would be disagreeable to the Proprietary. Many supply bills were framed by the Lower House "to save appearances" and throw the odium of rejecting them upon the administration, thereby making it appear, to use the Governor's words, "that it is entirely owing to the Government of Maryland and Pennsylvania being in the hands of Proprietors that money for His Majesty's Service is not so readily granted in these Provinces as in other Colonies."[2] Notwithstanding Sharpe's prediction of the approaching fulfillment of the proverb "which tells us that after a Storm cometh a Calm," the Lord Proprietary was dubious of the attitude of the Assembly toward him. This is clearly evinced by the base scheme which Calvert now proposed to Sharpe.

It was a design for bribing the Assembly, his plan being to repress a "Turbulent and Malevolent Spirit in the Lower

---

[1] Sharpe Cor., I., 401.
[2] Sharpe Cor., II., 179.

House of the Assembly." After advising Sharpe to be careful of his appointments to the Council, the "chief strength and support of his Lordship's rights," he explains that nineteen out of twenty of the Representatives of the people consult their own interests; "therefore by throwing out a Sop in a proper manner to these noisy animals it will render them not only silent, but tame enough to bear stroking and tractable enough to follow any directions that may be thought fit to be given to them."

Calvert's scheme was not to bribe the leaders but to buy off their followers. It is briefly as follows: Of the fifty-eight members of the House he would find "baits" for thirty. These "baits" were to be offices in the gift of the Administration, as the fourteen sheriffs' places, and others. At the beginning of each Assembly, which continued for three years, a majority of the members of the House were to be quietly promised an office on the expiration of their terms, provided they were favorably disposed toward the Proprietary and voted as the Administration dictated. By such a plan the Proprietary government hoped to silence "the pretended patriotic Spirit and clamour of the Lower House, and secure the harmonious working of the various branches of the Provincial Government like unto the wheels of a clock." Numerous details are prescribed in Calvert's letter[1] for the perfecting of his scheme. The essence of it only is sufficient for our purpose, that is, to reflect the character of the Proprietary at this time. Governor Sharpe's reply to this proposition illustrates well the integrity and firmness of a man who has been much misrepresented. While admitting it to be good policy to reward those who manifested a good disposition toward the government, he proves the utter impracticability of the scheme proposed. "Scarcely a member in the House," says the Governor,

---

[1] A secret letter from Calvert to Sharpe. Sharpe Cor., II., 375-380 (from the Calvert Papers).

"would thank me for bestowing such Offices on themselves or their Friends even without its being made a Condition that they should . . . give only one Vote contrary to their Inclinations." The attempt to execute such a design would have rendered the Proprietary government more odious to the people than ever, and the enemies of the government would have prevented it by legislation, though it is exceedingly doubtful if any of the members could have been ensnared into sacrificing their popularity and reputations for any such consideration. Never, probably, in the history of the province was a more foolish suggestion made to its Governor. Sharpe makes this very plain to Frederick's secretary, and takes the opportunity of observing again that too much dictation on the part of the Proprietary and his friends in the matter of appointments had already greatly handicapped his administration.[1] The moral rebuke which Sharpe administers to Calvert is well worth quoting: "The only way . . . for His Ldp to obtain a solid and lasting Influence . . . is to appear steady and resolute, to reward as far . . . as it is in his Power those who behave themselves well, but never bribe any of those who endeavour to carry their Points by Violence to desist or forbear; Let His Ldp and those in Authority under him pursue such Measures as they will always be able to justify and in the End I will engage that a vast Majority of the Upper Class of People will become Friends to His Ldp and well wishers to his Govern't."[2] These indications point to the fact that the province was seeking, or meditating at any rate, relief from Proprietary rule. Had not the cessation of hostilities soon restored the equilibrium of the government, it is difficult to surmise what might have happened.

If we look away to Pennsylvania at this time we find a very similar state of affairs. In responding to appeals for

---

[1] Sharpe Cor., II., 426-431.
[2] Sharpe Cor., II.,430.

supplies the Assembly continued to tax the estates of the Proprietaries. This called forth renewed opposition from the latter, and the people became so highly incensed that steps were taken to do away with the Proprietary government. It was determined to petition the Crown to purchase the province from the Proprietors and make it a Crown colony. Franklin was again appointed the provincial agent to convey the petition and urge the measure before the Ministry in London. With that object in view he sailed for England, November, 1764. The rupture with Great Britain, however, culminating the next year in the Stamp Act, soon subordinated all other questions, and Franklin exercised an influence little anticipated, becoming not merely the agent of his own province, Pennsylvania, but really the representative and defender of all the colonies.

Though Maryland did not go so far as Pennsylvania, and indeed had little occasion to, yet the applause given to the acts of her sister province indicates that very little interference would have been sufficient to drive her to a similar step.

Down to this time there had been no desire on the part of the colonies for union or independence of England, and there was no concerted action before 1765 for such a purpose. The colonies were at variance in their government, and the long distances between centers of population had prevented much intercommunication. All unity of action was merely sympathetic coöperation for defense. Indeed, the colonies had no grievances against the English Crown except the Navigation Acts. Maryland, in fact, did not come into contact with the Crown, for the latter had no taxing power over the province. The provincials were so pleased with the overlordship of the Crown that they made the mistake of supposing that Maryland would be better off as a Royal colony than as a Proprietary colony. The Assembly's reception of the report of Maryland's two commissioners to the Albany Convention was significant: " We do not conceive those Gentlemen were intended or impowered to agree upon any Plan of a proposed Union of the several Colonies . . . of which one General Government may be formed in America". . . .

After the close of the French and Indian War Great Britain's oppression changed entirely the phase of colonial affairs. The Stamp Act was the first direct menace of the liberties of the colonies. Aside from mere economical considerations, Great Britain doubtless had strong motives for the passage of such an act,—a desire to revenge the tardiness of the colonies in the late war and to remind them of her supremacy over them; but it was soon seen that the ministers who had favored such measures had made a mistake and an undue assertion of authority. Union was now felt to be a necessity for the preservation of their liberties. All other disputes and grievances were laid aside for the time; the provincials united for resistance, and Franklin was put on the defensive in London. The French and Indian War had been a general preparation, and the provinces, despite the backwardness of many of them, had at least learned the lesson that coöperation was necessary in all international struggles, and the only effective method of opposing dangers which threatened all alike.

Maryland had learned the lesson too, and manifested her willingness to unite with her sister colonies at this momentous period. The province had developed a spirit of aggression and resistance to Proprietary rule. We have seen how jealously the Assembly guarded the revenues of the province, and how they opposed all attempts of the Proprietary to infringe their taxing powers when once acquired. Similar attempts by Parliament to interfere with the "franchises" and "liberties" of the colonies finally led to their independence.

THE JOHNS HOPKINS PRESS,
BALTIMORE.

I. **American Journal of Mathematics.** S. NEWCOMB, Editor, and T. CRAIG, Associate Editor. Quarterly. 4to. Volume XIV in progress. $5 per annum.

II. **American Chemical Journal.** I. REMSEN, Editor. 8 nos. yearly. 8vo. Volume XIV in progress. $4 per volume.

III. **American Journal of Philology.** B. L. GILDERSLEEVE, Editor. Quarterly. 8vo. Volume XIII in progress. $3 per volume.

IV. **Studies from the Biological Laboratory.** H. N. MARTIN, Editor, and W. K. BROOKS, Associate Editor. 8vo. Volume V in progress. $5 per volume.

V. **Studies in Historical and Political Science.** H. B. ADAMS, Editor. Monthly. 8vo. Vol. X in progress. $3 per volume.

VI. **Johns Hopkins University Circulars.** 4to. Volume XI in progress. $1 per year.

VII. **Johns Hopkins Hospital Bulletin.** 4to. Monthly. Volume III in progress. $1 per year.

VIII. **Johns Hopkins Hospital Reports.** 4to. Volume III in progress. $5 per volume.

IX. **Contributions to Assyriology, etc.** Vol. I ready. $8.

X. **Annual Report of the Johns Hopkins University.** Presented by the President to the Board of Trustees.

XI. **Annual Register of the Johns Hopkins University.** Giving the list of officers and students, and stating the regulations, etc. *Published at the close of the academic year.*

ROWLAND'S PHOTOGRAPH OF THE NORMAL SOLAR SPECTRUM. New edition now ready. Set of ten plates, mounted. $20.

THE OYSTER. By William K. Brooks. 240 pp. 12mo.; 14 plates. $1.00.

THE TEACHING OF THE APOSTLES (complete facsimile edition). J. Rendel Harris, Editor. 110 pp. and 10 plates. 4to. $5.00, cloth.

OBSERVATIONS ON THE EMBRYOLOGY OF INSECTS AND ARACHNIDS. By Adam T. Bruce. 46 pp. and 7 plates. 4to. $3.00, cloth.

SELECTED MORPHOLOGICAL MONOGRAPHS. W. K. Brooks, Editor. Vol. I. 370 pp. and 51 plates. 4to. $7.50, cloth.

REPRODUCTION IN PHOTOTYPE OF A SYRIAC MS. WITH THE ANTILEGOMENA EPISTLES. I. H. Hall, Editor. $3.00, paper; $4.00, cloth.

STUDIES IN LOGIC. By members of the Johns Hopkins University. C. S. Peirce, Editor. 123 pp. 12mo. $2.00, cloth.

NEW TESTAMENT AUTOGRAPHS. By J. Rendel Harris. 54 pp. 8vo; 4 plates. 50 cents.

THE CONSTITUTION OF JAPAN, with Speeches, etc., illustrating its significance. 48 pp. 16mo. 50 cents.

ESSAYS AND STUDIES. By Basil L. Gildersleeve. 520 pp. small 4to. $3.50, cloth.

A full list of publications will be sent on application.

Communications in respect to exchanges and remittances may be sent to The Johns Hopkins Press, Baltimore, Maryland.

The Friedenwald Co.

Printing,

Lithographing,

Wood Engraving,

Book Binding.

Baltimore, Eutaw and German Sts.

Baltimore, Md.

The Leading House of the Art Preservative in Baltimore.

Printers of The American Journal of Philology, American Chemical Journal, American Journal of Mathematics, Studies from the Biological Laboratory, Studies in Historical and Political Science, issued by the Johns Hopkins University.

ESTIMATES CHEERFULLY SUBMITTED.

PERIODICALS PUBLISHED BY

FELIX ALCAN

108 BOULEVARD SAINT-GERMAIN,

PARIS.

Revue Historique.

Edited by M. G. MONOD, Lecturer at the Ecole Normale Supérieure, Adjunct Director of the Ecole des Hautes Etudes.

17th Year, 1892.

The "Revue Historique" appears bi-monthly, making at the end of the year three volumes of 500 pages each.

Each number contains: I. Several leading articles, including, if possible, a complete thesis. II. Miscellanies, composed of unpublished documents, short notices on curious historical points. III. Historical reports, furnishing information, as complete as possible, touching the progress of historical studies. IV. An analysis of periodicals of France and foreign countries, from the standpoint of historical studies. V. Critical reports of new historical works.

By original memoirs in each number, signed with the names of authorities in the science, and by reports, accounts, chronicles and analysis of periodicals, this Review furnishes information regarding the historical movement as complete as is to be found in any similar review.

Earlier series are sold separately for 30 frs., single number for 6 frs., numbers of the first year are sold for 9 frs.

Price of subscription, in Postal Union, 33 frs.

Annales de l'Ecole Libre des Sciences Politiques.

Published tri-monthly by the coöperation of Professors and Former Pupils of the College.

7th Year, 1892.

Committee of publication: MM. BOUTMY, Director of the College; LÉON SAY, Member of the Académie Française, formerly Minister of Finance; A. DE FOVILLE, Professor at the Conservatory of Arts and Trades, Chief of the Bureau of Statistics in the Ministry of Finance (Treasury Department); R. STOURM, formerly Inspector of the Finances and Administrator of Indirect Taxes; AUG. ARNAUNÉ; A. RIBOT, Deputy; GABRIEL ALIX; L. RENAULT, Professor at the Law College of Paris; ANDRÉ LEBON, Chief of the Cabinet of the President of the Senate; ALBERT SOREL; PIGEONNEAU, Substitute Professor at the College de Paris; A. VANDAL, Auditor of the First Class.

The subjects treated include the whole field covered by the programme of instruction: Political Economy, Finance, Statistics, Constitutional History, Public and Private International Law, Law of Administration, Comparative Civil and Commercial Legislation, Legislative and Parliamentary History, Diplomatic History, Economic Geography, Ethnography. The Annals besides contain Bibliographical Notices and Foreign Correspondence.

Subscription in Postal Union, 19 frs.

Revue Philosophique de la France et de l'Etranger.

Edited by TH. RIBOT, Professor at the College of France.

17th Year, 1892.

The "Revue Philosophique" appears monthly, and makes at the end of each year two volumes of about 680 pages each.

Each number of the "Revue" contains: 1. Essays. 2. Accounts of new philosophical publications, French and foreign. 3. Complete accounts of periodicals of foreign countries as far as they concern philosophy. 4. Notes, documents, observations. The earlier series are sold separately at 30 frs., and at 3 frs. by number. In Postal Union, 33 frs. Subscriptions to be paid in advance.

Payment may be for the periodicals through postal orders. The publisher will allow all expenses for money orders to be charged to him.

THE AMERICAN JOURNAL OF ARCHÆOLOGY

AND OF THE

HISTORY OF THE FINE ARTS.

The Journal is the organ of the Archæological Institute of America and of the American School of Classical Studies at Athens, and it will aim to further the interests for which the Institute and the School were founded. It treats of all branches of Archæology and Art History: Oriental, Classical, Early Christian, Mediæval and American. It is intended to supply a record of the important work done in the field of Archæology, under the following categories: I. Original Articles; II. Correspondence from European Archæologists; III. Reviews of Books; IV. Archæological News, presenting a careful and ample record of discoveries and investigations in all parts of the world; V. Summaries of the contents of the principal archæological periodicals.

The Journal is published quarterly, and forms a yearly volume of about 500 pages royal 8vo, with colored, heliotype and other plates, and numerous figures, at the subscription price of $5.00. Six volumes have been published.

It has been the aim of the editors that the Journal, beside giving a survey of the whole field of Archæology, should be international in character, by affording to the leading archæologists of all countries a common medium for the publication of the results of their labors. This object has been in great part attained, as is shown by the list of eminent foreign and American contributors to the three volumes already issued, and by the character of articles and correspondence published. Not only have important contributions to the advance of the science been made in the original articles, but the present condition of research has been brought before our readers in the departments of Correspondence, and Reviews of the more important recent books. Two departments in which the Journal stands quite alone are (1) the *Record of Discoveries*, and (2) the *Summaries of Periodicals*. In the former a detailed account is given of all discoveries and excavations in every portion of the civilized world, from India to America, especial attention being given to Greece and Italy. In order to insure thoroughness in this work, more than sixty periodical publications are consulted, and material is secured from special correspondents.

In order that readers should know everything of importance that appears in periodical literature, a considerable space has been given to careful summaries of the papers contained in the principal periodicals that treat of Archæology and the Fine Arts. By these various methods, all important work done is concentrated and made accessible in a convenient but scholarly form, equally suited to the specialist and to the general reader.

All literary communications should be addressed to the managing editor,

A. L. FROTHINGHAM, JR.,

PRINCETON, N. J.

All business communications to the publishers,

GINN & COMPANY,

BOSTON, MASS.

MODERN LANGUAGE NOTES.

A MONTHLY PUBLICATION

With intermission from July to October inclusive.

DEVOTED TO THE INTERESTS
OF THE
ACADEMIC STUDY OF ENGLISH, GERMAN
AND THE
ROMANCE LANGUAGES.

A. MARSHALL ELLIOTT, *Managing Editor.*
JAMES W. BRIGHT, H. C. G. VON JAGEMANN, HENRY ALFRED TODD,
Associate Editors.

This is a successful and widely-known periodical, managed by a corps of professors and instructors in the Johns Hopkins University, with the co-operation of many of the leading college professors, in the department of modern languages, throughout the country. While undertaking to maintain a high critical and scientific standard, the new journal will endeavor to engage the interest and meet the wants of the entire class of serious and progressive modern-language teachers, of whatever grade. Since its establishment in January, 1886, the journal has been repeatedly enlarged, and has met with constantly increasing encouragement and success. The wide range of its articles, original, critical, literary and pedagogical, by a number of the foremost American (and European) scholars, has well represented and recorded the recent progress of modern language studies, both at home and abroad.

The list of contributors to MODERN LANGUAGE NOTES, in addition to the Editors, includes the following names:

ANDERSON, MELVILLE B., State University of Iowa; BANCROFT, T. WHITING, Brown University, R. I.; BASKERVILL, W. M., Vanderbilt University, Tenn.; BOCHER, FERDINAND, Harvard University, Mass.; BRADLEY, C. B., University of California, Cal.; BRANDT, H. C. G., Hamilton College, N. Y.; BROWNE, WM. HAND, Johns Hopkins University, Md.; BURNHAM, WM. H., Johns Hopkins University, Md.; CARPENTER, WM. H., Columbia College, N. Y.; CLÉDAT, L., Faculté des Lettres, Lyons, France; COHN, ADOLPHE, Harvard University, Mass.; COOK, A. S., Yale University; COSIJN, P. J., University of Leyden, Holland; CRANE, T. F., Cornell University, N. Y.; DAVIDSON, THOMAS, Orange, N. J.; EGGE, ALBERT E., St. Olaf's College, Minn.; FAY, E. A., National Deaf-Mute College, Washington, D. C.; FORTIER, ALCÉE, Tulane University, La.; GARNER, SAMUEL, U. S. Naval Academy; GERBER, A., Earlham College, Ind.; GRANDGENT, CHARLES, Harvard University, Mass.; GUMMERE, F. B., The Swain Free School, Mass.; HART, J. M., University of Cincinnati, Ohio; HEMPL, GEO., University of Michigan; HUSS, H. C. O., Princeton College, N. J.; VON JAGEMANN, H. C. G., Harvard University; KARSTEN, GUSTAF, University of Indiana, Ind.; LANG, HENRY R., The Swain Free School, Mass.; LEARNED, M. D., Johns Hopkins University, Md.; LEYH, EDW. F., Baltimore, Md.; LODEMAN, A., State Normal School, Mich.; MORFILL, W. R., Oxford, England; MCCABE, T., Johns Hopkins University, Md.; MCELROY, JOHN G. R., University of Pennsylvania, Pa.; O'CONNOR, B. F., Columbia College, N. Y.; PRIMER, SYLVESTER, Providence, R. I.; SCHELE DE VERE, M., University of Virginia, Va.; SCHILLING, HUGO, Wittenberg College, Ohio; SHELDON, EDW. S., Harvard University, Mass.; SHEPHERD, H. E., College of Charleston, S. C.; SCHMIDT, H., University of Deseret, Salt Lake City, Utah; SIEVERS, EDUARD, University of Tübingen, Germany; SMYTH, A. H., High School of Philadelphia, Pa.; STODDARD, FRANCIS H., University of City of New York; STÜRZINGER, J. J., Bryn Mawr College, Pa.; THOMAS, CALVIN, University of Michigan, Mich.; WALTER, E. L., University of Michigan, Mich.; WARREN, F. M., Johns Hopkins University, Md.; WHITE, H. S., Cornell University, N. Y.

Subscription Price $1.50 per Annum, Payable in Advance.

Foreign Countries $1.75 per Annum.

Single Copies Twenty Cents.   Specimen Pages sent on Application.

Subscriptions, advertisements and all business communications should be addressed to the

MANAGING EDITOR OF MODERN LANGUAGE NOTES,
JOHNS HOPKINS UNIVERSITY, BALTIMORE, MD.

American Economic Association.

PUBLICATIONS.

A series of monographs on a great variety of economic subjects, treated in a scientific manner by authors well known in the line of work they here represent.

Among the subjects presented are Coöperation, Socialism, the Laboring Classes, Wages, Capital, Money, Finance, Statistics, Prices, the Relation of the State and Municipality to Private Industry and various Public Works, the Railway Question, Road Legislation, the English Woolen Industry, and numerous other topics of a like nature.

The latest publication is that for January, 1892,—Vol. VII, No. 1,—entitled:

The Silver Situation in the United States.

By F. W. Taussig, LL. B., Ph. D.,

Assistant Professor of Political Economy in Harvard University

118 pages, 8vo. Price, Seventy-five cents.

Six volumes of these publications, containing thirty-six numbers, are now complete.

The volumes will be sent, bound in cloth, at $5 each; any two for $9; any three for $13; any four for $17; any five for $21; all six for $25, and including subscription to Vol. VII, $29. Unbound, $4 per volume. A few copies bound in half-morocco are offered at $5.50 each; any two for $10; any three for $14.50; any four for $19.00; any five for $23.50; all six for $28.

Annual membership $3; life membership $50.

Orders and remittances should be sent to the

Publication Agent, American Economic Association,
Baltimore, Md.

STUDIES IN HISTORY, ECONOMICS AND PUBLIC LAW,

EDITED BY

THE UNIVERSITY FACULTY OF POLITICAL SCIENCE OF COLUMBIA COLLEGE.

The monographs are chosen mainly from among the doctors' dissertations in Political Science, but are not necessarily confined to these. Only those studies are included which form a distinct contribution to science and which are positive works of original research. The monographs are published at irregular intervals, but are paged consecutively as well as separately, so as to form completed volumes.

The first four numbers in the series are:

1. The Divorce Problem—A Study in Statistics. By Walter F. Willcox, Ph. D. Price, 50 cents.

2. The History of Tariff Administration in the United States, from Colonial Times to the McKinley Administrative Bill. By John Dean Goss, Ph. D. Price, 50 cents.

3. History of Municipal Land Ownership on Manhattan Island. By George Ashton Black, Ph. D. Price, 50 cents.

4. Financial History of Massachusetts. By Charles H. J. Douglas. Price, $1.00.

Volume I. complete. Price, $2.00.

Other numbers will be announced hereafter.

For further particulars apply to

PROFESSOR EDWIN R. A. SELIGMAN,

COLUMBIA COLLEGE, NEW YORK.

SOCIAL ECONOMIST BUILDING.

COLLEGE
OF
SOCIAL ECONOMICS
34 UNION SQUARE,
NEW YORK.

GEORGE GUNTON, PRESIDENT.

THE COLLEGE was organized primarily to teach a system of Social Economics suited to American Citizenship.

The ACADEMIC COURSE includes, besides Economics, History, English Language and Literature, Modern Languages, some of the higher Mathematics, Physics, Chemistry, Parliamentary Law, etc. There is also a COMMERCIAL COURSE occupying one year.

The LECTURE COURSES by President Gunton embrace Popular Discussions of Economics.

The "SOCIAL ECONOMIST," a monthly magazine edited by President Gunton and Starr Hoyt Nichols, treats subjects allied to Economics. The price is 20 cents per copy or $2.00 per annum. Sold by all dealers. Sample copies free.

This institution having outgrown its former quarters, the large building represented above has been secured, where commodious Class Rooms and Lecture Hall are arranged; also Editorial Rooms for the "Social Economist." Tuition fees are low on account of a liberal endowment. Prospectus sent on application. Address

J. O. WOODS, Business Manager.

There will soon be issued from the Johns Hopkins Press of Baltimore, a work entitled

AMERICA:
Its Geographical History, 1492 to the Present,
By DR. WALTER B. SCAIFE,

which invites attention to the much-neglected borderland that unites history and geography.

Starting with the discovery of Guanahani in 1492, it shows, by reference to maps and writings of the sixteenth century, the gradual evolution of the Atlantic and Pacific coast-lines in the consciousness of Europe. The third chapter sketches the slow growth of knowledge in Europe regarding the vast interior of the American continents and of the polar regions. There is a full discussion of the historical uses and the theories as to the origin of the names America, Canada, and Brazil. The history of our border lines, national and state, then engages the writer's attention; who passes from that subject to the geographical work of the national government, in treating which he has been aided by much information furnished direct from the offices of the Coast and Geological Surveys. In a Supplement Dr. Scaife undertakes to prove, contrary to the general opinion, that the Mississippi River is not always or even usually to be understood when the Spanish geographers mention the Rio del Espiritu Santo. The work will be illustrated by phototypes made from photographs of the famous Weimar and other maps, taken specially for the author. The volume will be sold for $1.50.

NOTES SUPPLEMENTARY TO THE STUDIES.

The publication of a series of *Notes* was begun in January, 1889. The following have thus far been issued:

MUNICIPAL GOVERNMENT IN ENGLAND. By Dr. ALBERT SHAW, of Minneapolis, Reader on Municipal Government, J. H. U.

SOCIAL WORK IN AUSTRALIA AND LONDON. By WILLIAM GREY, of the Denison Club, London.

ENCOURAGEMENT OF HIGHER EDUCATION. By Professor HERBERT B. ADAMS.

THE PROBLEM OF CITY GOVERNMENT. By Hon. SETH LOW, President of Columbia College.

THE LIBRARIES OF BALTIMORE. By Mr. P. R. UHLER, of the Peabody Institute.

WORK AMONG THE WORKINGWOMEN IN BALTIMORE. By Professor H. B. ADAMS.

CHARITIES: THE RELATION OF THE STATE, THE CITY, AND THE INDIVIDUAL TO MODERN PHILANTHROPIC WORK. By A. G. WARNER, Ph. D., sometime General Secretary of the Charity Organization Society of Baltimore, now Associate Professor in the University of Nebraska.

LAW AND HISTORY. By WALTER B. SCAIFE, LL. B., Ph. D. (Vienna), Reader on Historical Geography in the Johns Hopkins University.

THE NEEDS OF SELF-SUPPORTING WOMEN. By Miss CLARE DE GRAFFENREID, of the Department of Labor, Washington, D. C.

THE ENOCH PRATT FREE LIBRARY. By LEWIS H. STEINER, Litt. D.

EARLY PRESBYTERIANISM IN MARYLAND. By Rev. J. W. MCILVAIN.

THE EDUCATIONAL ASPECT OF THE U. S. NATIONAL MUSEUM. By Professor O. T. MASON.

UNIVERSITY EXTENSION AND THE UNIVERSITY OF THE FUTURE. By RICHARD G. MOULTON.

These Notes are sent without charge to regular subscribers to the Studies. They are sold at five cents each; twenty-five copies will be furnished for $1.00.

ANNUAL SERIES, 1883-1891.

Nine Series of the University Studies are now complete and will be sold, bound in cloth, as follows:

SERIES I.—LOCAL INSTITUTIONS. 479 pp. $4.00.
SERIES II.—INSTITUTIONS AND ECONOMICS. 629 pp. $4.00.
SERIES III.—MARYLAND, VIRGINIA, AND WASHINGTON. 595 pp. $4.00.
SERIES IV.—MUNICIPAL GOVERNMENT AND LAND TENURE. 600 pp. $3.50.
SERIES V.—MUNICIPAL GOVERNMENT, HISTORY AND POLITICS. 559 pp. $3.50.
SERIES VI.—THE HISTORY OF CO-OPERATION IN THE UNITED STATES. 540 pp. $3.50.
SERIES VII.—SOCIAL SCIENCE, MUNICIPAL AND FEDERAL GOVERNMENT. 628 pp. $3.50.
SERIES VIII.—HISTORY, POLITICS, AND EDUCATION. 625 pp. $3.50.
SERIES IX.—EDUCATION, POLITICS AND SOCIAL SCIENCE. 640 pp. $3.50.

The set of nine volumes is now offered, uniformly bound in cloth, for library use, for $27.00. The nine volumes, with eleven extra volumes, twenty volumes in cloth, for $42.00. The eleven extra volumes (now ready) will be furnished together for $16.00.

All business communications should be addressed to THE JOHNS HOPKINS PRESS, BALTIMORE, MARYLAND. Subscriptions will also be received, or single copies furnished by any of the following

AMERICAN AGENTS:

New York.—G. P. Putnam's Sons.
New Haven.—E. P. Judd.
Boston.—Damrell & Upham; W. B. Clarke & Co.
Providence.—Tibbitts & Preston.
Philadelphia.—Porter & Coates; J. B. Lippincott Co.
Washington.—W. H. Lowdermilk & Co.; Brentano's.
Cincinnati.—Robert Clarke & Co.
Indianapolis.—Bowen-Merrill Co.
Chicago.—A. C. McClurg & Co.
Louisville.—Flexner Brothers.
San Francisco.—Bancroft Company.
New Orleans.—George F. Wharton.
Richmond.—J. W. Randolph & Co.
Toronto.—Carswell Co. (Limited).
Montreal.—William Foster Brown & Co.

EUROPEAN AGENTS:

Paris.—A. Hermann; Em. Terquem.
Strassburg.—Karl J. Trübner.
Berlin.—Puttkammer & Mühlbrecht; Mayer & Müller.
Leipzig.—F. A. Brockhaus.
London.—Kegan Paul, Trench, Trübner & Co.; G. P. Putnam's Sons.
Frankfurt.—Joseph Baer & Co.
Turin, Florence, and Rome.—E. Loescher.

THE REPUBLIC OF NEW HAVEN.
A HISTORY OF MUNICIPAL EVOLUTION.
By CHARLES H. LEVERMORE, Ph. D.

(*Extra Volume One of Studies in Historical and Political Science.*)

The volume comprises 342 pages octavo, with various diagrams and an index. It will be sold, bound in cloth, at $2.00.

PHILADELPHIA, 1681-1887:
A HISTORY OF MUNICIPAL DEVELOPMENT.
By EDWARD P. ALLINSON, A. M., AND BOIES PENROSE, A. B.

(*Extra Volume Two of Studies in Historical and Political Science.*)

The volume comprises 444 pages octavo, and will be sold, bound in cloth, at $3.00; in law-sheep at $3.50.

Baltimore and the Nineteenth of April, 1861.
A STUDY OF THE WAR.
By GEORGE WILLIAM BROWN,
Chief Judge of the Supreme Bench of Baltimore, and Mayor of the City in 1861.

(*Extra Volume Three of Studies in Historical and Political Science.*)

The volume comprises 176 pages octavo, and will be sold, bound in cloth, at $1.

Local Constitutional History of the United States.
By GEORGE E. HOWARD,
Professor of History in the University of Nebraska.

(*Extra Volumes Four and Five of Studies in Historical and Political Science.*)

Volume I.—Development of the Township, Hundred and Shire. Now ready. 542 pp. 8vo. Cloth. Price, $3.00.

Volume II.—Development of the City and Local Magistracies. In preparation.

THE NEGRO IN MARYLAND.
A STUDY OF THE INSTITUTION OF SLAVERY.
By JEFFREY R. BRACKETT, Ph. D.

(*Extra Volume Six of Studies in Historical and Political Science.*)

270 pages octavo, in cloth. $2.00.

The extra volumes are sold at reduced rates to regular subscribers to the "Studies."

The Supreme Court of the United States.
Its History and Influence in our Constitutional System.
By W. W. WILLOUGHBY, Ph. D.
Extra Vol. VII of the Studies in History and Politics.
124 pages. 8vo. Cloth. Price, $1.25.

The Intercourse between the U.S. and Japan.
By INAZO (OTA) NITOBE, Ph. D.,
Associate Professor, Sapporo, Japan.
Extra Vol. VIII of the Studies in History and Politics.
198 pages. 8vo. Cloth. Price, $1.25.

State and Federal Government in Switzerland.
By JOHN MARTIN VINCENT, Ph. D.,
Librarian and Instructor in the Department of History and Politics, Johns Hopkins University.
Extra Vol. IX of the Studies in History and Politics.
225 pages. 8vo. Cloth. Price, $1.50.

In view of the fact that the six-hundredth anniversary of the foundation of Federal Government in Switzerland is celebrated in 1891, this may be considered a timely book. The history and constitutional experiments of Switzerland have, however, a perennial interest for Americans, for in no other country do governmental institutions approach more closely, in form and principle, those found in the United States. The present work is essentially a study of modern institutions, but always with reference to their source and development.

Spanish Institutions of the Southwest.
By FRANK W. BLACKMAR, Ph. D.
Professor of History and Sociology in the Kansas State University.
Extra Vol. X of the Studies in History and Politics.
380 pages. 8vo. Cloth. Price, $2.00.

With Thirty-one Historical Illustrations of old Spanish Missions, etc., and a map showing the extent of Spanish Possessions in North America in 1783.

This work is a study of the Social and Political Institutions of Spain, as represented by the life of the Spanish colonists in America. A sufficient amount of descriptive history is given to relieve the subject from the monotony of abstract discussion and to substantiate all conclusions reached by the writer. The book treats of the founding of the Spanish missions in California, Arizona, New Mexico, and Texas, and portrays the civilization established by the padres, the social condition of the Indians, and the political and social life of the pioneers of the Southwest. It represents the government, laws, municipal organization, and life of the colonists. The movement of the civil, religious, and military powers in the "temporal and spiritual conquest," and the consequent founding of civic pueblos, missions and military towns are fully discussed.

There are thirty-one illustrations, chiefly historical. They reveal some of the most picturesque ruins of America.

Orders should be addressed to THE JOHNS HOPKINS PRESS, BALTIMORE, MARYLAND.

NEW EXTRA VOLUMES NOW READY.

An Introduction to the Study of the Constitution.

A STUDY SHOWING THE PLAY OF PHYSICAL AND SOCIAL FACTORS IN THE CREATION OF INSTITUTIONAL LAW.

By MORRIS M. COHN,
Attorney-at-Law.

250 pages. 8vo. Cloth. Price, $1.50.

The theory underlying this work is that Constitutions, whether written or unwritten, represent the institutional growth of social communities; especially that institutional growth which is revealed in the governmental structure and maxims, and the jurisprudence, of the given community.

The aim of the author has been to show with somewhat less detail than has been adopted in more voluminous productions, yet with sufficient breadth of outline, the general prevalence of constitutional institutions among peoples who have made any advance at all in political organization.

The illustrations of the subject have been taken principally from the fields of politics and jurisprudence, though when required, or when it seemed to the author appropriate, other sources were utilized.

THE OLD ENGLISH MANOR.

By C. M. ANDREWS, Ph. D.,
Associate in History, Bryn Mawr College.

280 pages. 8vo. Cloth. Price, $1.50.

This work is an attempt to reconstruct the village and manorial organization and life in England at the beginning of the eleventh century. The study is based largely on the well known documents *Rectitudines Singularum Personarum* and *Gerefa*, the latter of which has never before been used for historical purposes. In addition all Anglo-Saxon literature has been put under contribution, that the study might be as complete as possible. Such reconstruction has more than a merely antiquarian interest, for it relates to an important period of English economic history. It shows the complete isolation of local life, the preëminence of agriculture, and the secondary importance of craft and artisan work. It brings Anglo-Saxon farming methods into line with post-Norman and shows the tenacity of the old life and custom, crude and uneconomical as it was, uninfluenced to any great extent by the Norman Conquest. In the introduction the writer discusses the origin of the manor, suggesting points of view somewhat different from those ordinarily received by the Germanic school, but supporting, in opposition to Mr. Seebohm, the freedom of the village community.

www.ingramcontent.com/pod-product-compliance
Lightning Source LLC
Chambersburg PA
CBHW020304090426
42735CB00009B/1218